T0034097

Dian and the Gorillas

LEVEL THREE **1000 HEADWORDS**

OXFORD
UNIVERSITY PRESS

Great Clarendon Street, Oxford OX2 6DP

Oxford University Press is a department of the University of Oxford.
It furthers the University's objective of excellence in research, scholarship,
and education by publishing worldwide in

Oxford New York

Auckland Cape Town Dar es Salaam Hong Kong Karachi
Kuala Lumpur Madrid Melbourne Mexico City Nairobi
New Delhi Shanghai Taipei Toronto

With offices in

Argentina Austria Brazil Chile Czech Republic France Greece
Guatemala Hungary Italy Japan Poland Portugal Singapore
South Korea Switzerland Thailand Turkey Ukraine Vietnam

OXFORD and OXFORD ENGLISH are registered trade marks of
Oxford University Press in the UK and in certain other countries

This edition © Oxford University Press 2010

The moral rights of the author have been asserted

Database right Oxford University Press (maker)

First published in Dominoes 2003

2014 2013 2012 2011 2010

10 9 8 7 6 5 4 3 2 1

ISBN: 978 0 19 424827 3 BOOK
ISBN: 978 0 19 424785 6 BOOK AND MULTIROM PACK
MULTIROM NOT AVAILABLE SEPARATELY

No unauthorized photocopying

All rights reserved. No part of this publication may be reproduced,
stored in a retrieval system, or transmitted, in any form or by any means,
without the prior permission in writing of Oxford University Press,
or as expressly permitted by law, or under terms agreed with the appropriate
reprographics rights organization. Enquiries concerning reproduction
outside the scope of the above should be sent to the ELT Rights Department,
Oxford University Press, at the address above

You must not circulate this book in any other binding or cover
and you must impose this same condition on any acquirer

Any websites referred to in this publication are in the public domain and
their addresses are provided by Oxford University Press for information only.
Oxford University Press disclaims any responsibility for the content

Printed in China

ACKNOWLEDGEMENTS

The author and editors would like to thank Ian Redmond for his comments on the
manuscript.

The publisher would like to thank the following for permission to reproduce photographs: Corbis pp6,
41 (Zoologist Dian Fossey/Yann Arthus-Bertrand), 6 (Bone), 45, 82 (Mountain gorillas/Yann
Arthus-Bertrand), 58 (Dian Fossey/Yann Arthus-Bertrand); Getty Images pp iv (Monkey),
6 (Trap/Chris Windsor); Ian Redmond pp iv (duiker), 32, 51, 61, 69; Magnum Photos pp1,
78 (Professor Louis Leakey/Ian Berry); National Geographic Image Collection pp5, 12,
13, 15, 16, 79 (Alan Root), 6 (tents), 26, 29, 35, 36, 53, 71, 72, 81, 83 (Robert I. Campbell),
19 (Michael Nichols), 21, 22, 77, 80 (Dian Fossey); OUP pp iv (Elephant/Photodisc), iv
(Young chimp/Photodisc), iv (Rhino/Corel), iv (Giraffe/Photodisc), iv (Tiger/Photodisc), iv
(Orangutan/Corel), iv (Zebras/Photodisc), 6 (Young chimp/Photodisc), 6 (Mountain Gorilla/
Photodisc), 7 (Forest/Digital Vision), 25 (Leaf detail/Photodisc), 38, 39 (Palm leaf/Photodisc),
46 (Camera/Ingram), 63 (Silverback gorilla/Corel), 70 (Gorilla in tree/Photodisc); R.I.M.
Campbell p3 (Sanwekwe/Bob Campbell); TopFoto pp9 (Dian Fossey/Topham/AP), 68 (Dian
Fossey with her book/Topham/UPP).

Cover: Rex Features (Dian Fossey in Rwanda/SIPA PRESS)

DOMINOES

Series Editors: Bill Bowler and Sue Parminter

Dian and the Gorillas

A True Story

Norma Shapiro

Norma Shapiro (1946–2004) was born, and lived most of her life, in Los Angeles, California. She was one of the co-authors of *The Oxford Picture Dictionary* and gave many training sessions for teachers of English both in the USA and overseas.

OXFORD
UNIVERSITY PRESS

BEFORE READING

1 **Dian Fossey is famous for her work with gorillas. Tick the other animals you think she sees in Africa.**

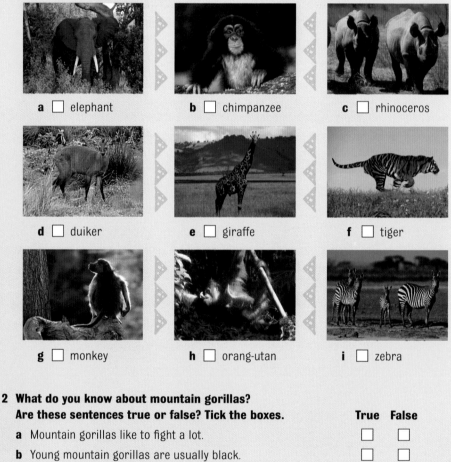

a ☐ elephant   **b** ☐ chimpanzee   **c** ☐ rhinoceros

d ☐ duiker   **e** ☐ giraffe   **f** ☐ tiger

g ☐ monkey   **h** ☐ orang-utan   **i** ☐ zebra

2 **What do you know about mountain gorillas?**
Are these sentences true or false? Tick the boxes.

		True	False
a	Mountain gorillas like to fight a lot.	☐	☐
b	Young mountain gorillas are usually black.	☐	☐
c	Old mountain gorillas become grey in colour.	☐	☐
d	Mountain gorillas usually live alone.	☐	☐
e	Mountain gorillas are difficult to find in the forest.	☐	☐
f	Mountain gorillas never eat plants.	☐	☐
g	Mountain gorillas are fully grown when they are about fifteen.	☐	☐

·CHAPTER 1·
Meeting the gorillas

duiker a small
animal with long
legs that eats
plants and can
run fast

anthropologist
someone who
studies the history
of different groups
of people

bone a hard white
thing inside the
body of an animal
or person

D ian Fossey had been in East Africa for a few weeks and had met many new animals with strange names, like **duikers**. She had also seen animals like giraffes and elephants that she had read about when she was a child. She had travelled many miles and seen many wonderful things, but she was not ready to go home – not yet. She wanted to meet the famous **anthropologists**, Mary and Louis Leakey.

Dian had no idea what she would say to Dr Leakey when and if she saw him. He and his wife Mary had discovered some of the oldest **bones** of the first men and women. What did she have to offer them? She had done nothing in her thirty-one years as interesting as that. But Dian knew that perhaps Dr Leakey could help her live her dream, a dream she had never told to anyone, not even her closest friends.

The Leakeys were working in Tanzania. Dr Leakey was busy at work when Dian arrived. She introduced herself, but he clearly did not have a lot of time for this tall American woman. She looked like another tourist to him.

'Dr Leakey,' asked Dian quickly, before he could turn back to his work, 'can you help me see some of the mountain gorillas? I'm so interested in them!'

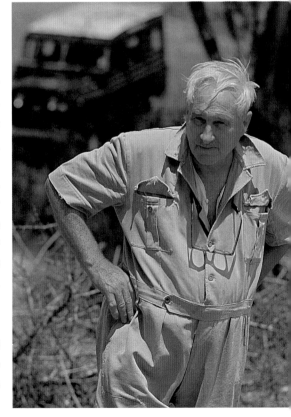

Dr Louis Leakey

1

'Why are you interested in them?' Dr Leakey looked at her closely. 'You're not one of those people – those tourists – who just wants to have their photo taken with King Kong, are you?'

'What? King Kong? Oh no, no, Dr Leakey. I know you helped Jane Goodall with her work on chimpanzees. And I've been reading about George Schaller and his study of mountain gorillas. Well, I just want to see the mountain gorillas. It's – it's a dream of mine.' Dian smiled as she spoke. Was she really saying this out loud? What must Dr Leakey think of her?

'Well,' answered Leakey, 'you'd have to go to the Congo to do that. But first, come with me. I'd like to show you something – the oldest giraffe bones in the world.' With that, Dr Leakey took Dian's hand and started walking up the nearest hill with her.

Dr Leakey took her to the edge of a deep hole. Dian wanted to show him that she was a serious student, so she started to climb down the side of the hole towards the bones – and fell. She hurt her ankle badly, and she had to be carried back to the **camp**.

At lunch, Mary Leakey told Dian, 'I think you'd better forget about the gorillas, my dear. They live high in the Virunga Mountains. It's a very hard climb, even with two good ankles. And the gorillas won't exactly be waiting for you. You may have to climb around for days, and even then . . .'

Dian looked at her ankle. It was turning from blue to purple. 'Please, Mrs Leakey, I've read so much about them. They are the closest animals to us . . . I must go, I really must. I'll **crawl** on my hands if I have to.'

'Well,' said Dr Leakey, 'you seem like the sort of person who could do just that. Good luck! And keep in touch!' And with that he left to go back to his giraffe bones.

Dian was not sure if Dr Leakey meant those last words, but she knew that she would remember them.

⁂

camp a place where people live in tents

crawl to move along slowly with the body close to the ground

It took Dian two weeks to reach the bottom of the Virunga Mountains. She stopped at the entrance to the Virunga National

Park. Since 1925 the gorillas had been **protected**. Nobody could kill or **trap** gorillas inside the park. Dian explained to the **guard** that she would stay no more than a week. He let her in, and she made the six-hour climb to a high, flat field where two of the mountains meet, the Kabara Meadow.

Staying in a **tent** at Kabara Meadow were two well-known photographers, Alan and Joan Root. They had been following the gorillas for a few weeks as part of their work. Dian could tell that they were not happy to see her – an American woman who had problems **breathing** and who had a hard time walking.

Dian waited to be invited to go with them to find the gorillas. Alan and Joan stayed in their tent, waiting for Dian to leave. One, two, three days went by. The Roots needed to get more photographs. Why wasn't the woman leaving? Finally, they agreed to take Dian with them.

The gorillas never stayed in one place very long. They moved around the mountain in small groups, looking for the plants that they liked to eat. Schaller, who had studied gorillas in the Virungas, had employed an African man, Sanwekwe, to help him **track** the animals. Sanwekwe was now working for the Roots.

'Nice to meet you, Miss Fossey,' he said smiling. 'Tomorrow, if we're lucky, you'll see a big mountain gorilla.'

'Oh, I hope so. I hope so very much.'

'To find gorillas, you must know how to look,' Sanwekwe said. 'Look out for the old day **nest** or night nest that they make from tree branches. Look out for the plants that they drop when

protect to save something from danger

trap to catch an animal in something; something to catch animals in

guard someone who watches people going into or out of somewhere

tent a small house made of cloth that you can take with you when you move

breathe to move air into and out of your chest

track to look for and follow animals

nest a bed that animals make to sleep or rest in

Sanwekwe

they eat – gorillas don't eat all of the plant. And look out for smelly new **dung**, too.'

Dian smiled. 'Good. I'll help look for smelly new dung.'

Sanwekwe returned the smile. An American who will look for dung! he thought. He liked this woman.

The next morning Dian was out of bed early. She went to the edge of the camp and stood quietly, staring out. There was a circle of clouds around the mountain above her, the air was full of **mist**, and the ground under her feet was wet and shiny. It was quiet, but her heart was beating fast. Where was life taking her?

Finally they started out, Sanwekwe first, then the Roots carrying their cameras, then Dian. The climb seemed almost impossible – straight up the mountain, through the forest, thick with trees and branches and leaves. For hours they climbed. Sanwekwe cut through the trees with his big knife, but the thick branches hit Dian's face, her arms, her legs. She was frightened too. Although she didn't tell anyone, she was always afraid of being high up.

Suddenly Sanwekwe stopped. He held up his hands – silently asking everyone to keep quiet and still. There was a rich, strong animal smell in the air around them. Then they heard wild cries, getting louder and louder. *Eeea! Eeea!! EEE-AA!! EEEE-AAA!!* Over and over again. Dian's legs were shaking. Then came a low **thump** and then another. *Thump! Thump!! THUMP!! THUMP!!*

Sanwekwe turned to them and beat his chest with his fists to explain the noise. Then he put his finger to his lips telling Dian to be quiet. Dian had never heard anything like this. But still she could see nothing. In front of her was a wall of green.

Alan, Joan and Dian waited for the cries and chest-beating to stop. Then they moved slowly forward, staring straight ahead, until they saw through the branches what seemed like a family – a very large family – of great mountain gorillas staring back at them. Their big hairy bodies stood tall, their **fur** shone deep black in the morning mist.

dung food that has passed through the body of large animals

mist a thin cloud near the ground

thump a low banging noise

fur the hair on an animal's body

Dian didn't know who was more surprised – her or the gorillas. But the gorillas didn't run away. One even moved closer to watch Alan get his camera ready. A few climbed the trees to get a better look at these new visitors. One broke branches off a tree while another wildly beat his chest again and ran into the forest.

Dian couldn't move. The Roots took their photographs moving around under the trees, but she just stared at the most beautiful animals in the world. 'Are we so very different?' she thought.

Deep inside her she knew that one day she would return to these mountains – to be with these animals again.

READING CHECK

Tick the boxes to complete the sentences.

a Dian meets Dr Leakey because she . . .

1 ☑ wants to ask him about mountain gorillas.

2 ☐ is interested in giraffe bones.

3 ☐ wants to take a photo of him.

b Near the Leakeys' camp Dian . . .

1 ☐ breaks her ankle.

2 ☐ hurts both ankles badly.

3 ☐ falls down a deep hole.

c In the Virungas Dian meets . . .

1 ☐ George Schaller.

2 ☐ Sanwekwe, a man who is good at finding wild gorillas.

3 ☐ two famous park guards.

d The photographers Dian meets . . .

1 ☐ invite Dian to go with them at once.

2 ☐ wait for Dian to go away.

3 ☐ are unhappy to see Dian and ask her to go away.

e Sanwekwe tells Dian to look for . . .

1 ☐ old gorilla nests up in the trees.

2 ☐ new gorilla dung.

3 ☐ new plants that the gorillas have put in the ground.

f When Dian sees the mountain gorillas for the first time, she is . . .

1 ☐ with the Roots and Sanwekwe.

2 ☐ all alone.

3 ☐ frightened and runs away.

WORD WORK

1 Match the words with the correct pictures.

a bone _tents_

b gorilla ....

c tents ....

d trap ....

e chimpanzee ....

f guards ....

2 Find words in the forest to complete the sentences.

a Sanwekwe tells Dian to look for smelly new gorilla ....dung.... on the ground.

b Dian visits the Leakeys in a .... in Tanzania.

c Dian has problems .... when she climbs mountains.

d Sanwekwe helped Schaller to .... animals.

e The gorillas rest in .... during the day.

f The Leakeys are .... working in Africa.

g Early in the morning the air is full of ....

h Most young gorillas have black ....

i Dian can hear the loud .... that gorillas make.

j Gorillas are .... animals – no one should kill them.

gund
mpac
gnihtbrae
ktarc
stesn
opornathgolssti
stim
ruf
sphutm
orpdettec

GUESS WHAT

What do you think happens in the next chapter? Tick three boxes.

a ☐ Dian goes to work in a zoo in the United States.

b ☐ Dr Leakey meets Dian again in America.

c ☐ The Roots write to Dian asking her to come to Africa.

d ☐ Dian writes a lot about the gorillas.

e ☐ Dian goes back to the Virungas to stay.

f ☐ Dian meets Sanwekwe again.

·CHAPTER 1·
The long wait

Dian returned to her home in Louisville, Kentucky. Her diary had grown very thick during the two months in Africa, and she had a suitcase of photographs. She wanted to return as soon as possible, but she had no money. Africa would have to wait.

She started working again at the Kosair Children's Hospital. Some of the children there had learning problems and almost never spoke. She tried to find out what each one needed. She watched them without staring, and helped them, but never hurried them. She knew it could take a long time for them to accept her.

One boy, Peter, never smiled. Other teachers had lost all hope that he could ever learn to talk, but not Dian. Every day she sat near him, and played very slowly with a **puzzle**. Some days he turned his head – almost looking at her. One morning, after several months, she found he had finished the puzzle for her. 'Quick hands!' she said to him.

Soon after that, he began to smile – and talk. 'I'm Quick Hands,' he said. It had taken eight months. 'I knew it would happen,' thought Dian. He needed time, that was all.

At night she wrote in her diary. She also wrote stories about the gorillas and sent them to newspapers. The gorillas had so many enemies – **poachers** who wanted to kill the adults and sell their babies to **zoos**, **cattle herders** whose cows destroyed the plants the gorillas ate – and people who wanted to make things out of their heads, hands and feet just to show their friends. There were probably fewer than five hundred gorillas in the Virunga Mountains. 'Who is going to save them?' she asked herself.

After several months, a Louisville newspaper **published** one of her stories with her photographs. Dian sent the story to her mother in California. People liked her story, and the newspaper

puzzle a picture in many pieces that you must put together

poacher someone who kills or steals animals

zoo a place where people can see wild animals from different countries

cattle herder someone who takes cows to different places to eat

publish to put a piece of writing in a newspaper or a book

published another. Dian hoped this would help the gorillas.

She also wrote a lot of letters, not just to her mother, but to a man she had met in Africa named Alexie. Alexie liked Dian very much. Some of his family lived in Africa and some lived in the USA. He was now a student in Indiana.

One day Dian's friend Mary stopped by to talk with her after work. Mary worked with Dian and also knew Alexie.

'You must be so happy,' said Mary. 'I hear Alexie is ready to marry you. That's better than going back to your gorillas.'

'Perhaps he'll come to Africa with me.'

'I don't think he wants to go to Africa now. He has to finish school here, Dian.'

'Well, maybe I have a job there!' Dian replied, angrily.

At Louisville

But a job in Africa was only a dream. For the next few years, Dian worked. She and Alexie talked about getting married, but the time never seemed right.

One day she read in the newspaper that Dr Leakey was coming to Louisville to speak. Dian could not believe her good luck. She hoped he would remember her.

The room was full of people when Dian arrived. She stayed in the back. At the end of his talk, she went up to him.

He looked at her. 'Dian, isn't it? Please wait a moment.'

Did he say 'Dian'? Did he remember her name? No, that's not possible, she thought.

He spoke to a lot of other people, and then smiled at Dian. She gave him a notebook full of her stories. He looked at them quickly, stopping at the beautiful photographs of gorillas.

'Wonderful,' he said. 'Can we meet tomorrow? I only have an hour, but we must talk. Come to my hotel – around nine.'

'Yes, yes. I'll be there!' she said almost dropping her notebook.

⌂ ⌂ ⌂

The next day Dian met with Dr Leakey at his hotel. 'Dr Leakey,' she began, 'that week in the Kabara Meadow was the most important week of my life.' She told him about her time with the Roots and with Sanwekwe. She told him about each gorilla in the family and how each was different. She told him about their chest-beating and the sounds they made. 'It was hard to come home, Dr Leakey,' she added.

'Well,' Dr Leakey said suddenly. 'Would you like to return? I'm looking for someone to study the gorillas. By studying them we can learn more about us. I think you're just the person!'

'That's what I believe, but surely you want a man who . . .'

'A man? Oh, no, Miss Fossey. Women are much better at this. They don't just look at the animals, they see them.'

'But are you sure you really want me? I work with children. I love animals but I've never really studied them.'

'I've talked to many people who want this job. Some already know something about gorillas. But this work isn't about what you know. It's more about who you are. I chose Jane Goodall to study chimpanzees, and she's been there for six years. I think you're the right person – and I've never been wrong yet!'

⌂ ⌂ ⌂

Everyone thought Dian was crazy. Alexie might find someone else. Dian was already thirty-four. Would she have another chance of finding a husband? She wrote to Alexie and told him she was not leaving him for ever. This was something she had to do. She hoped he understood.

Saying goodbye to the children at the hospital was more difficult. Peter still didn't speak to any other teacher.

'Why are you going?' he said to her on her last day. He put his head down on his desk and began to cry.

'The gorillas have no one to speak for them,' she replied. 'They need someone very badly right now.'

'Will I still be Quick Hands?'

'Of course. I'll tell Mary about your new name.'

When he looked up he gave a smile. 'Tell Mary, sometimes Peter is like a gorilla without words.'

Dian put her arms around him. 'I'll tell her.'

⁂

Dian left Louisville and went to stay with her parents in California. She was waiting to hear from Dr Leakey. It was taking him a long time to get the money for Dian's **research**.

Months went by. Dian spent her time studying Swahili, a language that was spoken in the Congo. She was worried the journey to Africa would never happen – and she was smoking a lot. And then she caught a very bad cold and went to bed with a **fever**.

One morning, her mother brought her some letters and a glass of orange juice. 'Drink this,' she said. 'When you feel better you can get another job, a real job.'

This is a real job, Dian thought as she looked at the letters. There was one from Dr Leakey. She opened it and read:

> We have the money! Can you be here by Christmas?
> I hope you've bought clothes and medicine.
>
> *Louis Leakey*

She had only a few days! Shaking with fever, she began to pack.

On December 15, 1966, Dian left for Africa with three very full suitcases, her typewriter, paper, four cameras, and enough film to take hundreds of photographs. At last she was going to study the only mountain gorillas in the world.

research studying something carefully to find out more about it

fever when you get very hot because you are ill

READING CHECK

Put these sentences in the correct order. Number them 1–9.

a ☐ Dian studies Swahili.

b ☐ Dian goes to stay with her parents in California.

c ☐ Dian gets a letter from Dr Leakey inviting her to Africa.

d ☐ Dr Leakey asks Dian to meet him at his hotel.

e ☐ Dian reads in the newspaper about Dr Leakey coming to Louisville.

f ☐ Dian shows Dr Leakey a notebook full of gorilla stories and photos.

g ☐ One of Dian's stories is published in the newspaper.

h ☐ Alexie and Dian talk about getting married.

i ☐ Dian starts working at a children's hospital in Louisville.

WORD WORK

1 Find words from Chapter 2 in the puzzle.

pub *cat*
poa *zo*
os *lish*
tle *sea*
chers *re*
fe *ed*
ders *ver* *rch* *her*

2 **Use the words in Activity 1 to complete these sentences.**

a A Louisville newspaper p͟u͟b͟l͟i͟s͟h͟e͟d͟ some of Dian Fossey's stories.

b Sometimes _ _ _ _ _ _ _ _ kill gorillas to sell their hands and feet.

c Sometimes baby gorillas are sent to _ _ _ _.

d _ _ _ _ _ _ _ _ _ _ _ _ _ are a problem because their cows destroy the plants that the gorillas eat.

e Dr Leakey asks Dian to go back to Africa to do some _ _ _ _ _ _ _ _ on gorillas.

f Dian goes to bed with a _ _ _ _ _ _.

GUESS WHAT

What do you think happens in the next chapter? Match the people with the sentences.

Alan Root	**a** . . . invites some people to help Dian in Africa.
Alexie	**b** . . . goes shopping with Dian in Nairobi.
Dr Leakey	**c** . . . travels with Dian to the Virunga National Park.
Jane Goodall	**d** . . . is good at telling Dian where the gorillas are.
	e Dian gives a handsome gorilla the name '. . .'.
Joan Root	**f** Dian understands how to get near the gorillas by thinking
Peter	of what she did with . . ..
Sanwekwe	**g** . . . shows Dian how to take notes on animals.

·CHAPTER 3·
Back to Africa

'Dian, Dian, over here!'

Dian was at the airport in Nairobi, Kenya. She looked around to see who was calling to her.

Suddenly Dr Leakey was there. 'Hello! Hello! You look great.'

'Dr Leakey! Thanks. I may look great but I need some sleep.'

'Sleep? Oh no, no. There's so much to do. Come, come with me. I must show you what I bought for you.'

Dr Leakey took Dian over to an old, sad-looking Land Rover. It had no windows and the seats looked hard. 'Get in and drive it around. This is the only car that will get you over African roads.'

'Now? But I don't know . . .' began Dian.

'Now!' said Dr Leakey pushing her in.

Dian turned the key. The car jumped around like a chicken with a broken leg. Dian wanted to cry.

'Good, good,' Dr Leakey shouted after her. 'You'll do better in a week or two!'

Dr Leakey had invited Jane Goodall, and Alan and Joan Root to help her. In two days Jane taught Dian how to take notes on animals and how to keep her notes in order. Joan Root took Dian shopping for food and other things.

Finally it was time for Dian to leave Nairobi. 'I'm ready!' Dian said, pushing the last box into the Land Rover.

'You may be ready, but are they ready for you?' said Alan.

'Who? The gorillas?' asked Dian.

'I'm not talking about the gorillas,' said Alan. 'I'm talking about the park **officials**. They may not let you in. You need the right papers. I hate to say this, but you're a woman and . . .'

'I'm not going to kill the gorillas – I'm going to study them!'

But Dr Leakey knew Alan was right, so he sent him with Dian.

official a person who decides important questions

It was a five-day drive to the park entrance. When they arrived, Dian started to explain to the park guard why she was there.

'Excuse me, Sir,' the guard said to Alan, pretending not to hear Dian. 'We have no papers for this woman. We haven't heard anything about her research. What is she trying to do? She can stay a week, but . . .'

Dian started to speak but Alan spoke first. Africa was a different place, he was trying to tell her. Let me talk. Dian understood and stayed quiet. Finally everything was arranged. She could stay in the park for two years.

The **trail** to Kabara Meadow was exactly as Dian remembered it. Sometimes they had to push between trees and **bushes** as they climbed, sometimes they were in open fields. When they reached Kabara Meadow, Alan and the **porters** put up tents, and arranged everything else in the camp. They even dug toilets.

Two days later Alan left. Dian couldn't say thank you or even goodbye. She was afraid that if she spoke at all she could very easily ask him to take her back. Crying silently, she watched him start down the trail. That night she **typed** letters to friends and listened to her radio. That only made her feel even more alone.

Dian on the trail

Sanwekwe, the tracker who had helped Alan and Joan, arrived four days later. Dian almost **hugged** him. She told him she was ready to track gorillas as soon as he unpacked his things. Maybe work would take away her feelings of loneliness.

It didn't take long before Sanwekwe and Dian found a group of gorillas. But before Dian could get out her camera, they disappeared into the forest.

trail a narrow road through wild country

bush a small tree

porter someone who carries bags for you

type to write something with a typewriter

hug to take lovingly in your arms

Climbing

'They smell us,' said Sanwekwe.

'Perhaps I should wear a **perfume** they like,' replied Dian, smiling for the first time since Alan had left.

Sanwekwe was good at telling Dian where the gorillas were, but he couldn't take away their fear of people. Poachers, hunters and even cattle herders had reasons for hurting them. How could Dian tell them she was a friend?

At first she tried hiding behind bushes. She couldn't see much, but in time they got used to her smell and didn't run away. She listened to their sounds – how the **females** called to their children, how the **males** frightened other animals away. She listened to their eating sounds, their playing sounds – some fast and loud, some slow and soft.

'This isn't enough,' she told Sanwekwe one day. 'I'm going to climb this tree. They won't see me in the branches.'

Dian began climbing. When she was two metres up she couldn't move any more. Sanwekwe started to laugh.

'Sh-h-h! You'll frighten them away!' Dian said.

'You must come down,' Sanwekwe said in a low voice.

'No. I think I'll be able to see them from the top.'

'If you don't fall and break your neck.'

'Sh-h-h! Help me a little, please, before they all leave!'

Sanwekwe gave Dian a push and up she went.

Finally Dian reached the top and looked through the branches. She hoped at least one or two of the gorillas were still there.

Yes, the gorillas were still there. But they weren't playing, they weren't eating, they weren't making noises. And they surely

perfume
something with a nice smell that you put on your skin

female an animal that can make eggs or have babies

male an animal that cannot make eggs or have babies

weren't afraid of her. The family was just staring up at her. 'This is a good show!' they seemed to say. 'What else can you do?'

When she came back down the tree, Sanwekwe had a big smile on his face. 'What are you going to do now?' he asked. 'You can't do all of your studying from the tops of trees.'

🏔 🏔 🏔

Dian tried out lots of different things to interest the gorillas. Although it was hard to climb with a heavy bag, she carried cameras, magazines, a notebook, and pens. She sat as close as the gorillas **allowed**, her head down, but watching carefully. She remembered Peter and the puzzles and she sat quietly near the gorillas, never staring at them, never even looking their way.

She thought it would help if they could see her as one of them. She pretended to eat wild **celery** the same way they did – breaking it into pieces, letting some drop from her mouth. She walked like they did – using her legs and her hands, but on her **knuckles**. She called this 'knuckle-walking' in her notes.

In the evenings she looked at her photographs and began to write about the gorillas. An old female with a very flat nose became No Nose. A handsome young male became Alexie. Dian wondered what the real Alexie would think of that. Soon she named all the gorillas she saw. She now understood more than she had ever thought possible. Her dream was coming true.

🏔 🏔 🏔

Six months later, a letter arrived:

Dian Fossey
It is dangerous for you to stay in the Congo.
There is a lot of fighting. You must leave the
park immediately.
Director, Virungas National Park

Dian had no choice. In six hours she packed up her camp. She cried all the way down the mountain.

---

allow to let somebody do something

celery a vegetable with long white and green sticks that you can eat without cooking

knuckle the place where two finger bones join together

ACTIVITIES

READING CHECK

Match the sentences with the people.

a **JOAN ROOT** …

b *Jane Goodall* …

c *Dr Leakey* …

d **ALAN ROOT** …

e Dian …

f Sanwekwe …

1 shows Dian how to take notes on animals.
2 tells Dian she needs the right papers to enter the Virunga National Park.
3 feels very lonely after Alan leaves.
4 meets Dian at Nairobi airport.
5 arrives at the park four days after Alan has left.
6 helps Dian to buy food and other things.
7 gives Dian an old Land Rover.
8 talks to the park guard for Dian.
9 helps the porters to put up tents in Dian's new camp.
10 helps Dian up into a tree.
11 gives all the gorillas names.
12 gets a letter saying it is dangerous to stay in the Congo.

WORD WORK

Correct the boxed words in these sentences.

a At night Dian used to tyre letters to her friends. ……type……
b Dian nearly bugged Sanwekwe when she saw him. ……………
c Pale gorillas frighten other animals away. ……………
d Feminist gorillas call to their children. ……………
e Dian remembered the train to Kabara Meadow very well. ……………
f Sometimes they had to push through trees and rushes as they climbed the hill.

……………

g Gorillas like eating wild salary. ……………
h Gorillas don't usually allot people to get close to them. ……………
i When they arrived, Alan and the porkers put up the tents. ……………
j Dian tried walking about on her buckles. ……………
k The park officers were more of a problem than the gorillas. ……………
l People sometimes use perfect to make themselves smell nice. ……………

GUESS WHAT

What do you think happens in the next chapter? Tick the boxes.

a ☐ Dr Leakey . . .
☐ Sanwekwe . . . tells Dian to go and study other animals outside Africa.

b Dian tells him that she wants to study . . .
☐ chimpanzees.
☐ gorillas.

c On the wall of her tent Dian has some photos of . . .
☐ gorillas.
☐ Alexie.

d Dian is surprised when she gets a visit from . . .
☐ Dr Leakey.
☐ Alexie.

·CHAPTER 4·
Karisoke

Because the fighting in the Congo was so bad, it took Dian a few weeks to get across the **border** into Uganda. She then flew to Nairobi where Dr Leakey met her.

'Well, all is not lost,' Dr Leakey said. 'You've learned a lot about tracking and watching wild animals. You can begin a study on the **orang-utans** in Borneo. I understand they're the same as . . .'

'Orang-utans the same as gorillas? The same?' Dian cried. 'No animals are the same. You've never met Alexie. He's really gentle. And No Nose. She's a wonderful mother. Then there's . . .'

Dr Leakey stopped her. He had heard these names before. Although he had never been to Kabara, Dian had written many letters to him. 'Just tell me, what can you do?' he asked.

'I can continue working with the gorillas!'

'And how are you going to do that?' Dr Leakey asked, knowing she would have some kind of answer.

'Gorillas don't know about borders. Part of the Virunga Mountains are in Rwanda. There's no war there. I met a Belgian woman, Alyette de Munck, who's lived in Rwanda for a very long time. She knows everything about the people and the mountains. She believes in what we're doing. She knows that . . .'

And this was when Dr Leakey realized that he could never say 'no' to Dian.

🔺🔺🔺

Dian started searching in the Volcanoes National Park in Rwanda. After a few days she found what she was looking for – new gorilla dung. Yes, the gorillas were also in Rwanda.

With Alyette and several porters helping her, Dian made camp close to Kabara Meadow, but across the border in Rwanda. It was in a flat valley between two mountains, Mount Karisimbi and Mount Visoke, so she named her research centre Karisoke. At

border where two countries meet

orang-utan a large orange-haired animal that comes from the same family as humans and gorillas

3,000 metres, it was not as high as Kabara Meadow but just as rainy, cold, and beautiful. There were trees and **bamboo** plants around the sides of the mountains.

Before dark on the first night, September 24, 1967, Dian heard a loud but friendly *thump – thump – thump*. A gorilla was beating his chest nearby in the forest. She fell asleep in her small tent as happy as she had ever been. She did not know that by the end of the next day she and Alyette would be angry with each other.

※ ※ ※

Dian had invited Alyette to go tracking with her. Dian thought perhaps they would be able to find the gorilla she had heard the night before. They had been gone over three hours, half crawling through a thick forest. Both women were tired. They had just found gorilla dung and Dian was looking at it very carefully.

'There's so much to learn from it,' Dian said to Alyette. 'Look. See the **flies** on it. When you find flies on dung like this, that means it's at least eight hours old. And look at the colour . . .'

'Stop!' said Alyette, turning her head away and laughing.

Suddenly, Dian put her finger to her lips. 'Sh-h-h! Listen.'

Soft crying came through the bushes. Dian followed the sound, Alyette behind her. A young duiker was caught in a trap of bamboo sticks and **ropes**. When the animal had walked across the bamboo, a rope had caught its leg.

A duiker in a trap

Dian was hot with anger. 'Look at this! Look at this!' she screamed, cutting at the ropes with her knife.

Alyette watched Dian silently.

'It's OK. It's OK,' Dian said to the frightened animal as she let him go. 'Your family's waiting for you.'

Alyette didn't say a word. Dian looked straight at her. 'What? What are you thinking?'

'There are people who live here, Dian, the Batwa. They've been hunting here for hundreds of years. That's how they get food for their families. That's all,' said Alyette.

'That's not all, Alyette. Hunting isn't allowed in this park. What chance do the animals have with these traps? The poachers have so many ways to kill them. They dig **pits** and cover them with leaves, they take long pieces of bamboo, like knives, and . . .'

'This is Africa. Without hunting, the people will die.'

'If no one protects the animals, they'll be gone for ever. This is the last place in the world for the mountain gorillas. The Batwa can go somewhere else.'

'It's not so simple, Dian. All of Africa is poor.'

'I'll tell you this, Alyette. Gorillas are caught in traps that the Batwa leave for duikers. Every time anyone from Karisoke finds a trap, we must destroy it.'

The two women started walking back to camp, the silence heavy between them. Without Alyette's help there would be no Karisoke. But she had to destroy the traps to save the gorillas.

Digit

Getting everyone to destroy traps, tracking a new group of gorillas that Dian called Group 4, (she had studied three groups in Kabara) and keeping her tent dry, kept Dian very busy.

Her favourite gorilla was a young male, four or five years old, who was still very playful. Gorillas become adult when they are about fifteen. Once when she was looking at him through her **binoculars**, she saw that one of his fingers was damaged. She named him Digit which means finger, and put a photograph of him on her wall next to the others.

Every night Dian typed her notes. One night, as she was finishing, she heard a friendly voice. 'Who's this?' it said.

Dian turned to see Alexie, the real Alexie, looking at Digit's photograph. She had not seen him in over a year although they had written to each other. She didn't know he was in Africa.

Dian couldn't speak for a time. 'What are *you* doing here?' she finally asked.

Suddenly there was a noise outside the tent. Three trackers were screaming her name. She ran outside and Alexie followed. The trackers had been checking some trails for traps when they found the body of a young gorilla who had fallen into a pit trap. Its hands and feet were gone. Someone had bought them because they looked good on coffee tables in America and Europe.

'Let me take you away from all of this,' said Alexie after they were back in her tent.

'What you are talking about? This is my life.'

'Very well, then. We'll get married. I'll move up here for one year. You can finish your research and then we can go back to the States together.'

'I don't need to be married, Alexie. I need to get rid of the poachers who are making all these traps.'

Alexie could see fire in her eyes. But he was very worried.

'I grew up in Africa, Dian, I know the people. They have different ways to hurt you. The poachers will use **black magic** on you if they don't like you.'

'Black magic? Don't be stupid! I'm not afraid of black magic.'

'It's really dangerous, Dian. And I feel sorry for you if you don't understand,' he warned her.

The next day Alexie left Karisoke. He felt that maybe he would never see Dian again, but he promised to send her something that would frighten the poachers away from her gorillas.

black magic something that makes bad things happen in a way that you can't understand

READING CHECK

Correct seven more mistakes in the chapter summary.

Nairobi

Dian goes to ~~California~~ to meet Dr Leakey. He wants her to go to Borneo to study

chimpanzees. Dian says 'no'. She wants to work with gorillas in Rwanda with the help of

a Belgian woman, Alyette de Munck. Dian's new camp is between the lakes Karisimbi

and Visoke, so she calls her centre Karisoke. It is 3,000 metres high, a bit lower than

Kabara Meadow. In the new centre Dian goes tracking gorillas with Alyette. Dian is

angry when she finds poachers' guns in the park, and decides that all the people

working at Karisoke must destroy them. Dian calls the first group of gorillas that she

tracks from Karisoke 'Group One'. One night Dian's friend Alexie arrives at her camp.

Soon after three trackers bring in a dead duiker. It has no head or feet because the

poachers have sold them for money. Alexie wants Dian to marry him. He says he will

move to Karisoke for a month but that then they must go back to the States. Dian is

more interested in stopping poachers than in getting married. Alexie leaves, saying

that he will send Dian something to frighten the poachers.

WORD WORK

Match the words in the leaf with the underlined words in the sentences.

a   Dian teaches Alyette to look at the <u>small black animals that can fly</u> on gorilla dung. ...*flies*...

b   Dian has to cross the <u>place where Congo and Uganda meet</u>. ....

c   At Karisoke there is <u>a tall plant made of hard green sticks</u>. ....

d   Sometimes the poachers dig <u>holes in the ground</u> which they cover with leaves. ....

e   They find a duiker with <u>a thick string</u> round its leg. ....

f   Looking through her <u>special glasses</u> Dian sees that one of Digit's fingers is damaged. ....

g   The poachers in Africa believe in <u>something that makes bad things happen</u>. ....

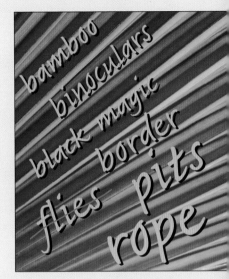

bamboo
binoculars
black magic
border
flies   pits
rope

GUESS WHAT

What do you think happens in the next chapter? Tick the boxes.

a   Alexie sends Dian . . .
   1   ☐ some guns.
   2   ☐ some mysterious music.
   3   ☐ some strange things to wear.

b   Dian brings . . .
   1   ☐ her mother from the States to live at Karisoke.
   2   ☐ two baby gorillas from a nearby town to live at Karisoke.
   3   ☐ the Roots from Nairobi to live at Karisoke.

c   Alyette . . .
   1   ☐ can't agree with Dian and stops helping her.
   2   ☐ doesn't always agree with Dian but goes on helping her.
   3   ☐ leaves Africa and goes back to Belgium.

·CHAPTER 5·
Two baby gorillas

Two weeks after Alexie left, a big box arrived for Dian from the United States. A porter brought it up the mountain and waited near her tent. Perhaps there was something small for him in the box, he thought. Dian had given him **candy** before.

She opened the box and smiled. 'Look,' she said turning to the porter. 'It's only a lot of **Halloween masks**. Here. Try one on!'

The porter covered his face and ran screaming from the tent. '*Sumu! Sumu!*' he cried.

'It's for Halloween! Just a children's holiday!' Dian shouted after him, but he was already too far away. She took out her dictionary and looked up *sumu*. It read: *Sumu – **Poison**. Also black magic.*

Porters on the trail

'Well,' she said to herself, 'Alexie knows more than I thought.' She put the masks under her bed and went back to work.

Soon Dian had a new **cabin**. Alyette gave it to her. Although the two women didn't agree about hunters, they were still good friends. Alyette wanted to help Dian and Karisoke.

During the next few months Dian found four more family groups. Uncle Bert, a **silverback** in Group 4, was her favourite. He protected the others.

Dian was seeing things few people had ever seen before. Uncle Bert often **tickled** Digit on his stomach. When it was sunny, Digit and a young female, Papoose, played on the hilly ground and chased each other up and down the biggest trees.

Dian wanted to show the world her discoveries, but she couldn't spend much time taking photographs, so she wrote to Dr Leakey.

candy sweet things to eat

Halloween the night of October 31st

mask something that you wear over your face

poison something that kills people or animals when they eat it

cabin a small wooden house

silverback an older male gorilla with silvery fur on his back

tickle to touch playfully with your fingers to make someone laugh

The world must know about the gorillas. Please, send me a photographer – someone who is not afraid of animals, or rain, or **mud**!

Dian

⟁ ⟁ ⟁

Several months later a porter brought a letter to Dian. She hoped Dr Leakey had found a photographer. But this letter was from a friend. Her smile disappeared as she read:

Dear Dian,
*A baby gorilla has been trapped by poachers. He is in a **cage** in Ruhengeri. The Park Director wants to sell him to a zoo in Germany, but he is very sick. He will die if you don't do something.*

Dian ran down the mountain and drove to Ruhengeri, the closest town to Karisoke. In the market place there was a crowd of children around a small cage. Dian's heart fell as she moved closer. A young male gorilla with sad dark eyes stared at her from the cage. He was sick with fever. Dian ran to the office of the Park Director, pushing open the door without knocking.

'Why do you have this baby gorilla?' she screamed. 'Tell me!'

The Park Director's voice was quiet but angry. 'It's for the good of the park. A zoo in Germany is paying a lot of money for him. The money will help the gorillas in the park.'

'How many gorillas did you kill just to get this one? How many?' Dian knew from watching Uncle Bert with his new baby that the poachers did not catch this young gorilla easily.

'Miss Fossey,' said the Park Director. 'The poachers will catch young gorillas with or without our help. At least this way we get some money for the park. To be honest, we can use it.'

In the end Dian and the Park Director agreed that she would take care of the baby gorilla until it could travel to Germany.

⟁ ⟁ ⟁

mud very wet ground

cage a box made of wooden or metal sticks to keep an animal in

Dian named the baby Coco and her small cabin was changed overnight for the new visitor. Her helpers went into the forest to find special food for him – the best fruit, the youngest sticks of wild celery – and big branches for his night nest.

Night and day Dian took care of Coco. Studying Uncle Bert, Digit and the others would have to wait. She had no time to go into the forests or to climb the **steep** trails.

Four weeks later another letter arrived. This time a baby female gorilla was sick. Dian went to Ruhengeri and took the baby back to Karisoke. She named her Pucker.

Every night as the babies slept, Dian wrote letters, as many as she could – to every animal **conservation** group she knew.

Karisoke Research Centre

We all want to save the gorillas. Please write to the zoo in Germany. Tell them not to take these young gorillas. Write to other zoos. Tell them gorillas should not be kept in cages.

After four weeks, Coco and Pucker were well and eating the same food as gorillas in the forests. Coco was jumping from Dian's bed to her table and back again. Pucker loved to hide things.

One day, Dian's shoes, a watch and a pack of cigarettes were missing. Coco and Pucker were both feeling better, but Dian was very tired. She opened her door and pushed the gorillas out, knowing they wouldn't leave the camp. 'Go on, play outside,' Dian said to both of them. 'I need some sleep.'

Coco didn't move.

'Go on, now. What a pain you are!'

'I am?' came back a deep voice.

Dian looked up. 'What . . .?'

'It's me, Bob Campbell. One photographer, ready to go,' said the tall man standing at her door.

Bob had been to Karisoke the year before. He had helped take

steep going up very high in a short time and difficult to climb

conservation saving the natural world

care of things when Dian had gone back for a short time to the *Dian, Coco,* United States. He was not only a good photographer of wild *and Pucker* animals – he was good with his hands, too.

'I guess you didn't get Dr Leakey's letter. I'm the photographer you asked for. I promise to be less trouble than that gorilla.' His smile was warm. His blue eyes were shining.

Dian wasn't really listening. 'Well, I'm leaving early tomorrow. I have to find a way to get these two back to the forest. They're not going to any zoo!' With that, she closed her door.

This was not the welcome he had expected.

I'm here to take pictures, he thought, I guess we don't need to talk much. He found his old tent and began to unpack.

A few days later, it was Dian who came to see Bob. She was crying. 'It's no use. They won't listen. If I don't let the babies go to the zoo, the park officials won't let me stay here.'

During the last two days for Coco and Pucker at Karisoke, Bob built a comfortable cage for them. Dian put healthy food inside it.

She couldn't stop crying on the day they were taken down the mountain. 'When is this going to end?' she thought. She needed a plan; without one the gorillas had no future. She just had no idea what that plan should be.

READING CHECK

Correct the mistakes in these sentences.

poachers

a Alexie sends Dian a present from the United States to help her frighten the ~~gorillas~~.

b Alyette tries to help Dian by selling her a new home to live in.

c Dian writes to Dr Leakey asking him to send her a secretary.

d Dian gets a letter asking her to save a baby zebra trapped by poachers in Ruhengeri.

e Dian is angry because the Park Director wants the animal to go to a zoo in England.

f Alyette agrees to care for Coco until he leaves for the zoo.

g Four weeks later Pucker, another sick adult gorilla, comes to stay at Karisoke.

h Bob Campbell hasn't been to Karisoke before Dr Leakey sends him there as a photographer for Dian.

WORD WORK

Use the words from the tracks to complete the sentences on page 31.

cage
candy
poison
steep *conservation*

cabin
masks *tickle* *mud*
silverback

a Alexie sends Dian some Halloween masks .

b The porter thinks that perhaps there is some .... in the box.

c The word *sumu* can mean 'black magic' or '.................' .

d Alyette gives Dian a new .... to live in.

e An older male gorilla is called a ....

f Dian watches Uncle Bert .... Digit's stomach with his fingers.

g She asks Dr Leakey to send a photographer who isn't afraid of rain or ....

h Dian goes to help a baby gorilla which is in a small .... in Ruhengeri.

i Some of the trails up the mountain are very .... and hard to climb.

j Dian writes about Coco and Pucker to every .... group that she knows.

GUESS WHAT

Match the first and second parts of these sentences to find out what happens in the next chapter.

a Dian likes . . .

b Dr Leakey talks about . . .

c Bob Campbell is interested in . . .

d Peanuts isn't afraid of Dian because she doesn't mind . . .

e Dian hates . . .

f Some magazines start . . .

g Alan, a schoolteacher in England, dreams of . . .

1 publishing Bob Campbell's gorilla photos.

2 having lots of smaller animals at Karisoke.

3 waiting for months to get nearer to him.

4 Dian going back to school.

5 going to Africa and doing what Dian did.

6 being a student in England.

7 making things move faster at Karisoke.

·CHAPTER 6·
A goodbye present

Soon after Coco and Pucker left, Dian had another animal visitor. She had already welcomed several smaller animals into the camp. There was a **puppy** called Cindy. There were also two chickens named Wilma and Walter, and a pair of black birds who came around every day for food.

On one of her visits into town, a poor man with a sick young **monkey** had come up to her. He wanted thirty dollars for the monkey. 'I don't need another animal to take care of,' thought Dian. Then she looked at the face of the monkey. Her eyes were nearly closed, her mouth moving up and down, waiting for food. Dian named the monkey Kima, which means monkey in Swahili.

Kima ate everything she wanted and played with Dian's things, but at least Dian knew she would never be sold to a zoo.

But Dian still couldn't sleep at night because she was thinking about the gorillas. She was not doing a good job of protecting them. The poachers weren't afraid of her. The Park Director surely wasn't afraid of her. She needed some help. Dian wrote to Dr Leakey. He wrote back quickly:

puppy a young dog

monkey a small animal with a long tail that can climb and lives in trees

Kima on Dian's hut

> You must show people that you know more about the gorillas than anyone in the world. I think you should go to Cambridge University to get your **doctorate** in the study of **primates**. Karisoke will become a study centre and university students can come to help you. Then the rest of the world will listen to you. Bob Campbell could probably take care of the camp while you are in Cambridge.

Dian wasn't sure about going back to school. And as for Bob Campbell, well, he had a lot to learn. He wasn't afraid of hard work. He didn't mind the long climbs. He didn't mind being wet all the time. His problem was that he wanted things to move faster.

He didn't understand the sounds she was making. Dian had explained to him that she learned many of them from Coco and Pucker. The little laugh, *aheh, aheh*, meant they were playing. The low, deep sound, *naroom, mauroom*, meant they were happy. She made these sounds to make the gorillas feel safe.

When Dian finally decided to go to Cambridge, Bob Campbell agreed to take care of Karisoke. But he thought Dian was taking a long time to get close to the gorillas. She usually went to a place where the gorillas could see her. Then she waited. She wanted to be sure they could climb nearby trees and look at her for a long time. Sometimes they saw her and sometimes they didn't.

Bob didn't like it that days were lost while the gorillas stayed away. And all those gorilla noises she made were unnecessary. He knew that Jane Goodall had put out bananas near her cabin, and the wild chimpanzees had come into her camp!

Finally he asked Dian about it. It was January 9, 1970. She was leaving the next day for Cambridge University. He knew she would be gone for three months.

doctorate a paper that students get after studying for many years

primate a large group of animals that includes gorillas, orang-utans, monkeys, and people

They were walking on the western side of Mount Visoke looking for Group 8. Dian liked Group 8. She felt that they **trusted** her more because they had no young gorillas to protect. Today, the clouds were moving across the sky and the air was misty. But the animals seemed to be hiding.

Bob Campbell was tired of waiting. 'Why can't you put out food for the gorillas – they'll learn to come to us.'

'Bob, what do you think will happen to them if they know that people will give them food?' This was a difficult climb and she was breathing hard. But that didn't stop her from getting angry at him. 'Think of the poachers! They'll put out a little food, too, and the gorillas will go for it! Do you think the poachers just want to take photographs?'

Bob Campbell knew when to stop. This was one of those times. Dian never changed her mind when once she'd decided to do something. Really, he didn't know how she did it. Her **lungs** were bad, she smoked too much and he knew she was afraid of high places. Sometimes when they reached the edge of a mountain, he could see her holding her breath as she moved along it.

'So,' he said, wanting to talk about something else. 'Where will it be today?'

Dian **pointed** to a group of trees at the bottom of Mount Visoke. 'I think they're down there. Do you remember what I told you about Peanuts? This is near the same place.'

Of course he remembered the story. It was during Dian's first summer at Karisoke. Peanuts, a young male gorilla, had been about five metres away from her. She didn't think he saw her. He was eating. But then he put down the branch he was holding and looked at her, almost staring. Dian usually didn't look back, but this time she did. They quietly looked at each other, five, ten, fifteen seconds. After some time, Peanuts went back to eating.

From that time, Dian knew Peanuts trusted her. It had taken ten months. It was worth every minute of waiting, she told him. You must be **patient**.

trust to feel safe with

lungs you have two of these in your chest to breathe with

point to show where something is with your finger

patient able to wait calmly for a long time

Dian and Bob had climbed up the mountain and now they were climbing down. Peanuts and the others weren't in the same place. Bob wanted to tell Dian that she should plan things a little better, but he knew that would just start another argument.

scratch to move the ends of your fingers quickly backwards and forwards on something

They climbed down a bit more. Finally Dian sat down and took out her notebook. They could both see three big dark shadows through the mist. One was much larger than the others.

Dian smiled. 'See,' she said. 'That is Group 8.' She pointed to the largest shadow. 'There's Rafiki.'

Rafiki was the oldest silverback in Group 8. His name meant *friend* in Swahili and he was Peanuts' father. His fur looked like a beautiful silver coat.

With Peanuts

'Look,' said Dian pointing to a smaller one. 'That's Peanuts coming out of his day nest.'

Bob Campbell was hiding behind the trees getting his cameras ready when Peanuts began to walk towards them. Dian moved away from the tree and pretended to eat some leaves that were on the ground. '*Naroom. Naroom mauroom, nauoom, mauroom,*' she said to the young gorilla.

Suddenly Peanuts was next to her. He sat down beside her and watched. His head moved from side to side. He was so much bigger than her. Dian didn't look straight at him.

She **scratched** her head. He scratched his. She scratched her neck. He did the same. She made the short playful sounds of Coco. '*Aheh. Aheh.*' He did the same.

Slowly she lay down on the ground with her arm reaching toward him, her hand open. She looked away from him. No one knows what Peanuts was thinking, but this time he was more brave. He reached over and put his hand in hers. It was the first time a wild gorilla had ever touched a person.

Bob Campbell could not believe what he was seeing. He took one photograph after another. Peanuts did not seem to mind.

A moment later the big gorilla stood up, beat his chest, made a *wraagh* noise and ran back to the others. 'See? See what I did!' he seemed to be saying.

Right then Bob Campbell knew that Dian was right. Peanuts had come over because he wanted to and because he felt safe with Dian. Bob could see that it would be wrong for the gorillas to trust anyone who gave them food.

For Dian it was a moment that changed her life.

The next day Dian packed and left for Cambridge University.

After a week in England, Dian wrote to Dr Leakey. She liked to be able to shop, she told him, and she liked to be able to eat fruit and vegetables every day. But she hated being a student again – and the weather in Cambridge was just awful. The sky was always grey, no clouds and no sun. There were too many people – and the noise! Not the sounds of birds, elephants and gorillas, but of loud cars and screaming trains. Just how necessary was this?

Dr Leakey wrote to Dian's **advisor** Robert Hinde. He had been Jane Goodall's advisor too. They made some changes. Now Dian only had to stay in Cambridge for a few months at a time. Surely

advisor a teacher at a university who helps someone to write about their research

that would be all right, wrote Dr Leakey.

Well, perhaps it would, agreed Dian. But the truth was that she didn't know anyone in Cambridge. Some days she spent all by herself. Yes, she went to classes and took notes and studied. But she was lonely. Everything she loved was in Karisoke.

Then one Friday morning, when the sun had come out, it seemed that everyone was friendlier than usual.

A fellow student, a young woman, stopped her after class. 'Now I know why you know so much about primates. Could we talk about them some time?'

'Well, I guess so,' said Dian, not sure what the woman meant.

Then another student, a man who was a little older than the others, sat next to her for the first time. 'So it's really you,' he whispered as class began. 'My name's Alan. I was a schoolteacher but my dream is to do what you did!'

'Do what?' Dian said.

Before the man could answer the **professor** began class, and they couldn't finish their conversation.

The day seemed to go like that. People were smiling at her, waving to her. Perhaps it's the nice weather, she thought.

When she arrived home there was a big **envelope** from the National Geographic Society waiting for her. She opened it and pulled out the latest *National Geographic* magazine. There, on the cover, with shining eyes and looking very sweet, were Coco and Pucker with Dian. Inside was the story about Dian and the gorillas – and Bob Campbell's photographs.

Now Dian understood why everyone was smiling at her. In one day she had changed from being Dian Fossey, university student, to being Dian Fossey, the woman who had become friends with wild gorillas. People wanted to get to know her. Some wanted to go to Karisoke. Well, if they wanted to work hard, they could.

Three months later with the first part of her time at Cambridge at an end, Dian returned to Africa. Now she needed students who could help her in her work.

professor an important teacher at a university

envelope a paper cover that you put a letter in

READING CHECK

Tick the boxes to complete the sentences.

a Dian buys Kima the monkey because . . .

   1 ☐ she needs to take care of more animals.

   2 ☑ she feels sorry for her and doesn't want her to be sold to a zoo.

b Dr Leakey wants Dian to study at Cambridge University . . .

   1 ☐ because he thinks she doesn't know enough about gorillas.

   2 ☐ to help the gorillas at Karisoke.

c Bob Campbell says he will take care of Karisoke while Dian is away . . .

   1 ☐ but Dian doesn't think he's ready to do that at first.

   2 ☐ and Dian agrees at once because he's so hard-working.

d Dian doesn't want to put down food for the gorillas because . . .

   1 ☐ she isn't interested in getting good photos of them.

   2 ☐ she doesn't want to make things easier for the poachers.

e Dian's advisor Robert Hinde says she can leave Cambridge every few months . . .

   1 ☐ so she can go back to Africa more often.

   2 ☐ because he had been Jane Goodall's adviser.

f Dian hates living in Cambridge because she doesn't like . . .

   1 ☐ the noise of cars and the bad weather.

   2 ☐ English food.

g When Dian's story is published in the *National Geographic* magazine people in Cambridge read it and are . . .

   1 ☐ more friendly because they know more about her.

   2 ☐ suddenly cold to her because she's become famous.

WORD WORK

Find words in the leaves to complete the sentences.

a Dian has a small puppy called Cindy.

b People and gorillas are _ _ _ _ _ _ _ _ .

pypup
tisrempa

c In the African language Swahili, Kima means _ _ _ _ _ _.

d Group 8 _ _ _ _ _ _ Dian because there are no babies.

e Dian gets near the gorillas because she is so _ _ _ _ _ _ _ _.

f When Dian _ _ _ _ _ _ _ _ _ _ her head, Peanuts does the same.

g Because Dian smokes, her _ _ _ _ _ are bad.

h Dian goes to Cambridge University to get a _ _ _ _ _ _ _ _ _.

i Dian's _ _ _ _ _ _ _ agrees she can go to Africa every few months.

j A teacher at university is called a _ _ _ _ _ _ _ _ _.

k Dian finds a big _ _ _ _ _ _ _ _ _ waiting for her at home.

GUESS WHAT

What do you think happens in the next chapter? Circle the names to complete these sentences.

a Bob Campbell
   Dr Leakey   arranges for Dian to speak about gorillas in Los Angeles.

b Bob Campbell
   Dr Leakey   makes a film about the gorillas.

c Dian falls in love with Bob Campbell.
                             Dr Leakey.

d Bob Campbell
   Dr Leakey   knows that he can't stay in Karisoke.

The image contains the words:
yomnek
rstust
tanepit
cascserth
gusln
rotatecod
odisarv
fersropofs
veepolen

·CHAPTER 7·
Back in Karisoke

Alan's dream was coming true. He was the schoolteacher who had sat next to Dian, and now he was going to take care of Karisoke when she returned to Cambridge.

Dian was happy Alan had agreed to come. She hoped she had chosen the right person this time. She promised herself she would be nice to him. She had even arranged for him to have a **salary** – Dian herself had never had a salary since she left Louisville.

△△△

Alan was not the first student to come to Karisoke. The first was Michael, a big tall Californian who had arrived at Karisoke in July, 1969. She remembered one of their first conversations. He was in his tent, putting away his things.

'I'm sure we'll get to know each other, but that's not important right now,' she began. 'The mountains are very dangerous for the gorillas. We need to know exactly how many gorillas there are, where they are, and how much they travel. We need to tell people how many have died. And you must learn all about gorilla dung—'

'Look, I just got here,' said the new student. 'Can't this wait?'

Dian didn't hear him. 'And the cattle herders. They're taking their cows all over the mountains. Those stupid cows are destroying just as many gorillas as the poachers!'

'I've never heard of fights between gorillas and cows. Who cares about cows?'

Was this boy listening? 'Who said they fight?' Dian shouted.

Michael stood up. This woman and her gorillas did not frighten him. 'Can you stop shouting and just explain it to me?'

Dian took a deep breath and spoke slowly. 'It's easy to understand. By walking on the plants that the gorillas eat, the cows destroy them. This means there is less food for the gorillas.

salary money that you get every month for your work

40

The herders aren't allowed to bring their cows inside the park, but of course they do!'

'I'm not a policeman. Surely there are park officials who take care of this.'

'Look. If we don't make a noise about it, the officials won't do anything,' her voice became very loud again. 'One of your jobs is to keep the herders and their cows out of the park!'

Michael left Karisoke after a month. He thought there were better ways to study gorillas than looking at dung, and he didn't want to chase herders or anyone else.

🛆 🛆 🛆

Dian was not unhappy he left. Yes, she needed students. But if she didn't get rid of the poachers and cattle herders she was sure there soon wouldn't be any gorillas to study.

Her Halloween masks weren't working any more. The last time the poachers were caught by her helpers she had put on a real show. She danced around the frightened men screaming at them. She held a **torch** and **scared** them with the fire. They began screaming at her – soon she heard the same word over and over again '*Nyiramachabelli!! Nyiramachabelli!!*'

torch fire on the end of a big stick

scare to make somebody feel afraid

Dian and her helpers with traps

She let them go. But she asked Rwelekana, one of her best trackers, 'What does this mean? What is *Nyiramachabelli?*'

'Maybe you don't want to know,' he said.

'Oh, come on. It can't be that bad!'

He knew he must not lie to her. 'It means *The old lady who lives in the forest without a man.*'

'This means I don't scare them, right? They think I need a man to protect me. Well, I don't!'

Perhaps she didn't, but the gorillas needed someone – or something – more than her. Her trackers found more and more traps, sometimes more than twenty a day. The cattle herders took their cows through the places the gorillas loved most. And the gorillas never fought back. They just moved farther and farther away searching for food. Something had to be done.

Dian thought for a long time before she came up with an answer. She had never hurt a living thing in her life. But if she didn't do something soon, the gorillas wouldn't **survive**. She was thinking about all of this when Alan arrived at Karisoke.

⏶ ⏶ ⏶

Dian was friendly to Alan when he arrived. He loved animals, and he had taught **biology**. That was a good start. She let him find out about camp life before she told him about the work. She told him how to get the things he needed and how to survive without being able to go to a market around the corner.

Then Dian took him to see the groups of gorillas. She taught him all of the gorilla sounds so that he could make them. She showed him how to track, how to look at dung and how to tell if the animals were sick or healthy.

But after all of that, Dian showed Alan her gun. 'Use it to protect the gorillas,' she told him. 'If we can't do that, there's no reason for us to be in these mountains.'

⏶ ⏶ ⏶

Finally Alan understood how to take care of Karisoke and Dian could leave. Dr Leakey had something for her to do on her way to

survive to live through difficult or dangerous times

biology the study of plants and animals

Cambridge. He had arranged for her to speak at a big party in Los Angeles. He wanted the people at the party to listen to Dian talk about the gorillas and then give money to his **organization**. Dian was worried. She knew she would have to talk for sixty minutes. What if the people were bored?

She brought with her beautiful **slides** of the photographs that she and Bob Campbell had taken. There on the **screen** in the big dark room were Uncle Bert and Aunt Flossie lying in the sun with Simba on Aunt Flossie's stomach. Uncle Bert's coat was shiny black. Simba was reaching up and pulling on Aunt Flossie's fur. Aunt Flossie was almost smiling.

There were photographs of Digit holding a sweet piece of tree branch and of Coco and Pucker climbing in some bushes. When Dian showed the slides of Peanuts, she told how he reached out to touch her. These, the largest primates in the world, looked no more dangerous than puppies.

Then Dian showed a slide of a young female gorilla whose hand had been caught in a trap. The hand was useless. It looked like a flat pocket with fingers. Dian explained how the gorilla didn't have a name because she was never seen after the photo was taken. How could she climb or take care of herself? Dian asked.

When Dian finished speaking no one said a word. It was so quiet, Dian thought everyone had fallen asleep. Then the lights went on. After that, everyone began to shout and **clap** and they didn't stop for a long time. Some people were crying as they clapped. Some asked her how they could give more money. Many promised to help her any way that they could.

Dian was really happy she had come to Los Angeles. She travelled on to Cambridge thinking that perhaps Digit, Peanuts, Simba and the others had a chance after all. She stayed in Cambridge for six months, studying as much as she could.

⁂

When Dian finally returned to Karisoke everyone came out to welcome her. They stood around her and many hugged her. They

organization a group of people working together for something

slide a small photograph that you show to people by shining light through it

screen something flat and white on which you show slides

clap to hit your hands together many times to show you are pleased

43

had tea ready, they wanted to tell her stories.

Mostly Dian felt wonderful. But she knew that the person who she really wanted to see was Bob Campbell.

Dian was thirty-nine years old. Maybe she wanted to be married, maybe not. She wasn't sure. But she knew that she was in love with Bob Campbell. She wanted him to stay at Karisoke forever. How could she tell him?

By now Bob had begun a new **project** at Karisoke. The people at *National Geographic* were so happy with the photographs, they wanted him to make a film of the gorillas. He was spending many days with them – much of the time alone. He was just like Dian when he was with them. The gorillas accepted him.

Dian's first night back she stopped by Bob's cabin. He had a lot to tell her. 'You were right, Dian. I'm getting things on film that I never thought were possible with wild animals. Digit was so funny today. Do you know what he did?'

Dian said nothing. Usually she loved to talk about Digit.

'You're quiet,' Bob said. 'Don't tell me you're **jealous**!' He laughed because, of course, that couldn't be true.

'Jealous? Yes, I think I am,' she said without looking at him.

'Well, don't be. Digit doesn't like me any better than you!' He started to laugh again, but Dian was not smiling.

'I want you to stay here. I want you to stay in Karisoke for always. I know I am not the only one in your life and I want to be.'

Now it was his turn to be quiet. He had photographed animals all over the world. He knew this was the most exciting work he would ever do. He loved Dian for allowing him into the lives of the gorillas. But his life was not in Karisoke.

Dian knew what his silence meant. Sadly, she went back to her cabin alone. For the next three months they worked together so he could complete the film. She was very busy, but she didn't know when she would be happy again.

project a piece of planned work

jealous feeling angry or unhappy because someone you like is interested in someone else

＊＊＊

Bob Campbell just had one more week in Karisoke. The film,

*Search for the Great **Apes***, was almost finished. Early one morning they went out to film Group 4.

Digit was pulling at some branches. Uncle Bert was tickling Cleo, his baby daughter. Aunt Flossie was making a day nest.

Dian and Bob slowly knuckle-walked towards the group. Bob got his film camera ready while Dian sat down near a tree. She pretended to be busy with her things. She took out her gloves, a notebook, a mirror, some film and arranged them next to her. She looked in the mirror and put it down. She opened her notebook and closed it. She put a pencil on top of her notebook.

Bob began filming her. Digit was close by. He was following everything with his eyes. He slowly knuckle-walked over and sat down next to Dian. Although Dian was tall, he seemed twice as big as her. Using his fingers as gently as possible, he picked up her glove. And then, like a young puppy, he smelled it. Dian did not move. She did not look at him. Digit picked up her pencil, then her notebook.

Group 4

Bob kept his camera on them. He was waiting for Digit to run away, but Digit lay down next to Dian. Soon he fell asleep.

Dian couldn't guess what Digit was thinking, but it was clear that he felt safe. Dian felt she was the most special person in the world. This is my life, she thought. Bob Campbell or no Bob Campbell, I can never leave Karisoke.

ape a group of animals; gorillas and chimpanzees are apes

READING CHECK

What do they say? Match the sentences.

1 By walking on the plants that the gorillas eat, the cows destroy them.

2 Digit doesn't like me any better than he likes you.

3 I want you to stay in Karisoke for always.

4 It means *The old lady who lives in the forest without a man.*

5 *Nyiramachabelli!*

6 Use it to protect the gorillas.

7 What is *Nyiramachabelli?*

8 I've never heard of fights between gorillas and cows.

a ⟦5⟧ the poachers shout to Dian.
b ☐ Dian asks her tracker Rwelekana.
c ☐ Rwelekana explains to Dian.
d ☐ says Michael, a new student from California.
e ☐ Dian explains to Michael.
f ☐ says Dian, as she shows her gun to Alan.
g ☐ says Bob Campbell to Dian.
h ☐ says Dian to Bob Campbell.

WORD WORK

On page 47 is a possible entry from Dian's diary. Use the words in the film in the correct form to complete it.

slide ape clap biology project jealous salary survive scare screen torch organization

I haven't had a **a)** ..salary.. since I left Louisville but money isn't important for me. The gorillas are important. Sometimes when I find poachers near Karisoke I hold up a **b)** .... in front of their faces and shout at them. I hope that it **c)** .... them. If I don't do something to help, the gorillas won't **d)** .... for long. Just before I left Africa, Alan arrived at Karisoke to look after things. He taught **e)** .... before, so I think that he'll be fine. Now I'm in America, trying to get some money for Doctor Leakey's **f)** .... I've got lots of **g)** .... of the gorillas with me and today I showed them on a **h)** .... to lots of people. They all **i)** .... when I finished speaking. My friend Bob Campbell is in Karisoke at the moment. He's starting a new **j)** .... while I'm away. It's a TV film called Search for the Great **k)** .... — all about how they live in the wild. I'm a bit **l)** .... of Bob. I'd like to be back in Africa now with the gorillas, not here in Los Angeles.

GUESS WHAT

What do you think happens in the next chapter? Tick the boxes.	Yes	No
a Dr Leakey dies.	☐	☐
b Karisoke becomes famous through Bob Campbell's work.	☐	☐
c Bob Campbell comes back to ask Dian to marry him.	☐	☐
d Lots of students want to come to Karisoke.	☐	☐
e Dian kills a cow.	☐	☐
f Dian burns a poachers' village to the ground.	☐	☐
g Dian starts to write a book about the gorillas.	☐	☐
h Digit kills a tourist.	☐	☐

·CHAPTER 8·
Poachers

After Digit fell asleep next to Dian, the fourteen gorillas of Group 4 made Dian feel as welcome as a sister. The little ones thought she was one of them and they climbed all over her. The older ones looked through Dian's hair for leaves and **insects** as they did with each other. Dian spent long days with them.

Dian wrote to Dr Leakey and told him all about Group 4 and how close she was to them. It was one of her last letters to him. In late 1972, Dr Leakey died. He had helped Dian start Karisoke and she promised herself that she would not forget him.

By 1973, through Bob Campbell's *National Geographic* film, Karisoke was famous. Students from many places, especially Cambridge, wanted to come there to study. There were many gorillas in the Virunga Mountains, and Dian had tracked ninety-six of them. It was a lot of work to track them all.

When new students arrived at Karisoke, they were told what to do. Yes, Dian said, you will study the gorillas. You will learn all about them – how they eat, where they sleep and how they play. You can have your own research. But most important, she told them, you will keep them safe.

The thought of even one of them getting hurt made Dian go crazy. She had lived in Karisoke for six years and she had done some awful things to protect the gorillas – things she never thought possible.

One time, she found some cows eating where Group 5 had been the day before. How many times had she warned the cattle herders? They knew that cows were not allowed in the park. And so Dian did the unthinkable. She took her gun and killed an animal – a poor cow whose only mistake was eating in the wrong place. The herder came to get the dead animal. Dian promised him she would kill one cow every day until the cows left the mountains

insect a very small animal with six legs

48

for ever. That night she wrote in her diary:

I hate myself for doing this. The poor cows just won't die, won't die. I can't stand seeing this.

The cattle herders left. A new Park Director agreed with Dian and helped keep the cows out of the park. For Dian, all her hard work had been worth it.

But the problems with the poachers only got worse. One rainy night, Dian was in her cabin looking through photographs of the different gorilla groups. She had taken so many pictures. She picked up one after the other. In one, Digit was holding and eating a thick branch. This picture had been made into a big **poster** and sent to conservation groups in many countries. There was also a picture of Puck, a baby from Group 5, looking through one of Dian's magazines. Dian couldn't stop herself from laughing as she looked at Puck's serious face 'studying' the magazine.

Suddenly there was a loud knock at the door. It was Nemeye and Ian. Nemeye was one of her African **staff**, and Ian was a student who cared about the gorillas as much as Dian. He, like Dian, believed there was a war going on in the Virunga Mountains – Dian and the students of Karisoke against the poachers and the cattle herders.

Ian's clothes were all muddy. His face was dirty and wet. He was very angry. 'Munyarukiko is doing it again, Dian. He and six other poachers were trying to get at Group 5. You know, we found thirty-five traps.'

Dian threw down the photographs. 'Tell me! Tell me! Did they get anyone?' she screamed.

'I think they wanted Poppy. But no they didn't get her.'

Dian loved Poppy – the newest baby in Group 5. 'Beethoven was there, of course?' she asked.

Beethoven was Poppy's father. He was the oldest silverback and he protected all of Group 5.

poster a large picture that people put on their walls

staff a group of workers

'Oh, yes!' said Ian. 'He was there. He screamed his wildest *Wraaagh* sound. It was louder than an airplane taking off. Brahms and Bartok followed behind him. They chased Munyarukiko and the others away. Really, Dian – how many times is this now?'

Dian couldn't answer. She was so tired of it all. It had been four years since Bob Campbell had left and Dian had tried everything. Every time a poacher was caught she did everything she possibly could to scare him. She had tied them up, she screamed and shouted and shot her gun over their heads. She used her Halloween masks and waved a big knife in front of their faces. This scared them, but not enough to stop them making traps and not enough to stop them stealing young gorillas.

Dian put on her jacket, took her gun and left with two of her staff. She told Ian to stay at the camp. He was already **exhausted**. Also, she knew she wanted to do something terrible and she didn't want the other students to hear about it.

They drove to the Batwa village where Munyarukiko lived with his wives and children. Dian shot her gun in the air. The women ran into their grass **huts** trying to protect their children.

'Go! Go away,' the women shouted.

'Not until Munyarukiko comes back!' Dian shouted.

One little boy of about four, Munyarukiko's son, came out of the hut alone. Dian **grabbed** him and gave him to Nemeye. 'Don't let him go,' she told him.

Then Dian went into the huts and started taking things out, making a big **pile**. 'If Munyarukiko doesn't come back, I'll burn it all!' she warned the women.

Dian waited, but not very long, before she lit the pile. The women screamed but Dian didn't stop.

When Munyarukiko still didn't return, Dian went crazy. 'Let's go! We're taking the boy!'

Nemeye was afraid, but he had to speak. 'You can't **kidnap** the boy, Miss Fossey. We can't do that.'

'We can and we will, Nemeye. Munyarukiko must learn what

exhausted very tired

hut a small, simple house

grab to take something quickly in your hand

pile a number of things put one on top of the other

kidnap to take as your prisoner

it feels like to have a son taken away from him. Do you think Beethoven feels any different?'

Nemeye wanted to say that Beethoven was a gorilla, and he didn't know how Beethoven felt. But Nemeye knew that the gorillas were like Dian's family. And he also knew that he had to obey Dian.

At camp, Dian fed the boy dinner and gave him a game to play with. She made sure he was warm and gave him chocolate candy. After a few days the boy was returned to his father.

Some of the people at Karisoke couldn't believe what had happened. Kidnapping a little boy? What did the boy do wrong? No gorilla was even hurt! They were angry at Dian and the feeling around the camp was terrible.

Problems with poachers at Karisoke

Dian did not worry about it. There had been many students, some who had left after only a few days. Who cared what these students thought? Some, like Ian, felt the same as Dian, although he was unhappy about some of the things she did.

But many others had heard about what had happened in the poacher village. They were also very angry with Dian. The park officials did not like Dian and her men trying to be policemen. That was *their* job. Some people at the National Geographic Society in Washington DC were afraid of what Dian could do next.

There was another problem. Many people, like those who came to hear Dian talk in Los Angeles, wanted to protect the gorillas. They were people who gave money to conservation groups. Some of these people thought that Dian Fossey had gone crazy. They had already heard so much. She used black magic and guns, she killed cows and tied up poachers with ropes. Now she was starting fires and kidnapping children. Worst of all, she didn't seem to understand that even poachers had families and children, and had to work to stay alive.

Even though there were other people who understood her – her African staff, the **Ambassador** to Rwanda from the United States, and some close friends – it seemed the world was against her.

Dian understood the gorillas better than any person. If she sat in one place they came to see her and rested nearby. The babies slept at her feet. Many of them, Uncle Bert, Digit, Macho, often came over to her and just stared into her face. Kweli, Uncle Bert's and Macho's new baby, came and played with her bag. If she felt angry and crazy, it was to protect them.

Dian wanted the world to know how loving these animals could be – just as they were, in the wild. She decided to write a book. She knew it would take a long time because she had so much to tell, but she felt maybe it would give the gorillas a chance.

☖ ☖ ☖

By Christmas, Dian's cabin was filled with papers. There were notes everywhere. Except for the big Christmas party which she

Dian at work

had every year, she was at her typewriter most of the time. There was so much to write.

She wrote about how the gorillas make night nests and day nests. She wrote about their food and where it is found. She wrote about how they travel and what kind of **footprints** they leave. She wrote and wrote and wrote.

The day after New Year's Day, Dian decided to take a walk. The sun was out, the air was cool. She could not stay inside. Ian and Nemeye were out looking for traps.

Suddenly Ian was in front of her on the trail. His eyes were dark. He was biting the side of his lip. Nemeye was farther back, looking at the ground. She knew as soon as she saw them that something awful had happened.

'Group 4?' she asked.

'Digit,' said Ian. 'He's been killed by poachers.'

In that moment, for Dian, the sun disappeared and her world turned black. Nothing, nothing, she felt, would ever be the same.

footprint the hole that someone's foot makes in soft ground when they walk

53

READING CHECK

Complete these sentences.

a   In 1972 ..Dr. Leakey.. dies, and Dian promises to continue the work in Karisoke.

b   In 1973 through Bob Campbell's .... Karisoke becomes famous.

c   One day Dian .... one of the cattle herders' cows to frighten them.

d   A group of .... try to catch the youngest gorilla in Group 5.

e   Dian goes to Munyarukiko's .... with her helper Nemeye.

f   She takes Munyarukiko's .... back to her camp for a day.

g   Many people start to say that Dian is ....

h   Dian decides to .... about her life with the gorillas.

i   On January 2nd Digit is ....

WORD WORK

1   **Find words from Chapter 8 in the puzzle.**

G	X	V	B	H	D	Z	X	K	V	F	K
R	P	W	P	O	S	T	E	R	E	H	D
A	M	B	A	S	S	A	D	O	R	I	Z
B	W	A	G	C	V	E	K	O	S	N	P
S	F	O	O	T	P	R	I	N	T	S	S
O	G	T	G	I	T	C	H	S	A	E	W
T	P	J	E	G	R	U	U	L	F	C	J
K	I	D	N	A	P	S	T	J	F	T	Y
C	L	S	Z	A	I	F	S	S	Z	S	B
T	E	X	H	A	U	S	T	E	D	S	R

2 Use words from Activity 1 to complete the sentences.

a Dian makes a photo of Digit into a ......*poster*........ .

b Nemeye is one of Dian's African ....

c The older gorillas of Group 4 look for leaves and .... in Dian's hair.

d When Dian goes angrily into the Batwa village the women there run into their grass

....

e Ian is .... after he comes back to camp to tell Dian about the poachers

attacking Group 5.

f Dian .... Munyarukiko's child with one hand and gives him to Nemeye.

g Nemeye doesn't think it's right to .... a child.

h Dian burns a .... of things in the Batwa village.

i The US .... to Rwanda understands why Dian does terrible things to

the poachers.

j You can track gorillas by looking for their .... in the mud.

GUESS WHAT

Make five sentences with these phrases and find out what happens in the next chapter?

a Dian and Ian tell

b A poacher tells

c Dian tells the police to take

d Park officials start

e Dian leaves Karisoke

f Dian that

g the world

h to bring tourists

i to teach

j Munyarukiko's man

k Munyarukiko's men killed Digit.

l in New York.

m about Digit's death.

n away from Karisoke.

o to Karisoke.

·CHAPTER 9·
Digit

Dian's first thought was for the other gorillas. 'Has anyone else in Group 4 been injured?'

She sent Ian to check and walked quickly back to her cabin. Once inside, she pushed the door closed, went to her desk and looked at her notebooks and papers. Her book wasn't important now. She knew it would take years before it was published. How many more gorillas had to die before then? None of the animals was safe.

Dian's heart was breaking. All afternoon she looked at her photographs of Digit. There were so many of them – pictures of him sleeping by her side, pictures of him studying her notebook and playing with Tiger and Bravado. She looked at pictures of Simba who was **pregnant** with Digit's first child. Digit had been the guard for the group. Now there was only Uncle Bert to protect Simba and the others. And the poachers would come again.

The next day six of the staff brought Digit's body back to the camp. They were afraid to tell Dian, afraid to hear her scream when she saw him. He had been cut in so many places.

Ian was not afraid of Dian. He knew how Dian felt because he felt the same way. He went to her cabin.

'Dian,' he called through the door, 'I have to talk to you.'

She let him into the cabin. Neither of them could sleep. They talked through the night.

'I don't want to tell anyone,' said Dian. 'No one in the world cares as much as we do.'

Ian knew that wasn't true. 'When people learn about Digit, they will send money,' he said.

'To who? To the park officials?' Now Dian was screaming. 'The park officials and the poachers are friends! The park officials will

pregnant with a baby inside her that will be born later

just use the money on themselves!'

It was true. Dian used to pay extra money to the park officials when they caught a poacher. More than once the park officials brought poachers to Karisoke. But after they got the money for their 'prisoners', they sometimes let the poachers go free.

'Maybe this time is different, Dian,' said Ian.

'Is it? I don't trust them at all!'

Ian thought for a moment. What Dian was saying was true. 'Maybe we can ask them to send money to us,' said Ian quietly. 'No, not to us. To a special **fund** in Digit's name. That way we can pay the men ourselves. We'll use it to stop the poachers.'

By morning Dian and Ian had decided on a plan. They wanted to tell the world about the death of this gentle animal. Ian went out and took photographs of Digit's body.

Dian wrote letters to as many people as she could – the President of Rwanda, the National Geographic Society, conservation groups and newspapers and magazines. She talked about the special fund. Soon it was named *The Digit Fund.*

Exhausted, she fell asleep as the sun went down.

Writing letters helped Dian feel a little better. But that ended soon. A few days later she heard one of her men running into the camp screaming, 'Poacher! Poacher!!'

This was the first time a poacher had come so close. There were no gorillas here, thought Dian. They must be looking for duikers.

Dian took her gun and ran out of her cabin, calling to Nemeye and the others. She saw the poacher run out of the camp toward the mountain. Dian shot her gun over his head. The poacher ran on and Nemeye and the others followed. Dian tried to run after them but she couldn't breathe. She couldn't see what was happening. Suddenly Nemeye came out from behind some trees holding a Batwa man by his arms.

Dian started to shout at him. 'You can't come into my camp! The duikers in my camp are . . .'

fund money used for something special

grave a hole in the ground where you put a dead body

Then she saw his shirt. It was old and yellow – and covered with dried blood. Too much blood from one duiker. It was Digit's blood.

They brought the man into camp. Dian and the men tied him up with a rope and kept him tied up all night. By the next day she had the information she wanted. This man and five others had killed Digit. Their leader was Munyarukiko.

Dian wanted to kill the man immediately. She wanted to go back to Munyarukiko's village and kill him. But she didn't. Instead, she sent a letter to the Chief of Police, not to the park officials. In the letter she told him she had the poacher who killed Digit. She told him to come soon before she did something terrible to the man. The Chief of Police came up to Karisoke and took the poacher away. In her diary, Dian wrote:

> *To let the man go was one of the most difficult things I have ever done in my life.*

After the Chief of Police left, Dian asked her men to dig a **grave** for Digit. He was buried at Karisoke near her cabin.

Digit's grave

Dian did not think that life for the gorillas could get worse, but she was wrong. A few weeks later, early in the evening, she and Ian were spending some time with Group 5. Coming back to camp, they heard loud voices on the trail. They were not expecting anyone, and the students knew better than to make so much noise around the gorillas.

'They should be near here,' they heard someone saying in French.

'I wonder if they will **growl** at us,' said another.

'I heard they will play with us,' said a third.

Who are these people? thought Dian.

Dian and Ian walked quickly toward the voices. As they came around some trees beside the trail, they saw them – a park guard with four Belgian tourists behind him. There was a tall man and a short man, an older woman and a young woman who looked like her daughter. They had cameras and binoculars around their necks. The park guard was trying to show them around.

'I'm sorry,' said Dian. 'Did you come to see the gorillas?'

'Oh, yes,' said the tall thin man.

'Well, they're eating right now,' said Dian in a too-sweet voice. 'Maybe this isn't a good time.'

'Who is this woman?' said the short man to the park guard.

Dian pushed the park guard before he could answer. 'Get out of here! What gives you the right to **disturb** these animals?' she screamed at him, her face red with anger.

'I'm sorry this is disturbing you,' said the tall man, trying to move past Dian. 'But we paid good money to see . . .'

Dian turned to the guard. 'You know that tourists must not come near the gorillas,' she shouted angrily.

'OK. You win this time,' said the guard. He turned to the tourists. 'Let's go,' he said to the Belgians.

'We climbed up for four hours . . .' said the older woman.

'And now you can climb back down!' said Ian.

The park guard turned to Dian. 'You will hear from the Park

growl to make a deep angry noise

disturb to stop someone from feeling calm

59

Director!' he said angrily.

'Oh, but he will hear from me!' said Dian as she pushed the tourists out of her way and started down the trail with Ian.

⁂

That night Dian wrote a very angry letter to the **Department of Tourism**. She knew that they wanted tourists to see the gorillas. They thought that tourists would spend a lot of money and this would help the Rwandan people. Dian did not agree.

Dian showed the letter to Ian. 'What do you think?' she asked.

'Dian, be careful,' he said after he read it. 'If you make the Rwandan **Government** angry, they can make life difficult.'

'Do you know what tourists will do to the gorillas? They will scare them and make them move – maybe right into the poacher's traps. The tourists will bring new **diseases** to the gorillas, diseases they will die from. I don't care how much money will come into Rwanda! No tourists are going to see my gorillas!'

'Please don't send it,' said Ian. 'What if the government throws you out of Rwanda?'

⁂

Dian, of course, didn't listen to Ian. But Ian was right. The official who read the letter was very angry. He wrote many letters himself. He sent them to important people saying that Dian was crazy. She was shooting guns at tourists now. What if she killed someone? And she didn't care at all about the Rwandan people. This was not her home. It was theirs.

Soon many of the people who had helped Dian were now asking her to leave Karisoke. Friends at the US **Embassy** in Rwanda and others at the National Geographic Society told her she needed time away from Karisoke.

In a way it was true. She did not go to see the gorillas anymore. She spent all of her time writing letters and organizing the work against poachers.

Still this wasn't enough. During the summer of 1978, poachers killed Uncle Bert and Macho trying to **capture** their baby, Kweli.

Department of Tourism an office that works to get more tourists to visit a country

government the people who control a country

disease illness

Embassy the office of an ambassador

capture to catch

Kweli was shot in the arm and died a little later. They all had graves at Karisoke, near Digit's grave.

One day soon after Uncle Bert was killed, Group 5 was eating at the edge of Karisoke. They had never been closer. One of the students came to her cabin.

'Dian,' she said. 'Come. Group 5 is the closest they have ever been. You won't have to climb. It is easy to see them now.'

Leaving for New York

But Dian stayed in her cabin. She was afraid that every visit with the gorillas would be the last one.

⏶ ⏶ ⏶

When Cornell University in New York offered her a teaching job, she knew she had to go. If she left Karisoke, she could finish her book. Lots of people would read it. Also she was always in pain from **hip** and back problems, and she couldn't breathe very well. Maybe her time at Karisoke was over.

Dian wanted Ian to stay at Karisoke and take care of the camp. She thought he was the only one who knew how to protect the gorillas. But Ian couldn't – he had hurt his wrist going after a poacher, and he needed time in a hospital. Another student agreed to stay at Karisoke.

It took over a month for Dian to pack up her cabin. She had lived there for more than eleven years. The staff cried as they helped her. Nemeye promised he would fight against the poachers. Dian and her dog Cindy walked down the mountain with several men carrying her suitcases and boxes. Some people thought she would never return.

hip the bone at the top of the leg

READING CHECK

Circle the words to complete these sentences.

a After Digit dies Dian
- burns her papers.
- cries.
- (looks at old photos of him.)

b Ian has the idea of using
- Dian's
- Digit's
- Simba's
story to get money.

c Dian gives the man who killed Digit to the police but really she
- wants to kill him.
- is sorry for him.
- wants him to learn to love gorillas.

d Dian shouts at a guard when she meets
- some Belgian tourists.
- a group of poachers.
- the Park Director in the park.

e Dian writes an angry letter about the tourists to the
- US Embassy in Rwanda.
- Rwandan Department of Tourism.
- *National Geographic* magazine.

f In the end Dian decides to go and
- teach in New York.
- kill Munyarukiko.
- finish her book in Karisoke.

g
- A student
- Nemeye
- Ian
agrees to take care of things while Dian is away.

WORD WORK

1 Find words in the monkey to complete the sentences.

growldisturbutbrave

capturesmhipembassywdiseasesepregnantgovernment

a Simba is <u>pregnant</u> with Digit's child when Digit dies.

b Dian starts a special …………………… in Digit's name to get money for the gorillas.

c Dian's men bury Digit in a …………………… near her cabin in Karisoke.

d Soon after Digit dies, Dian …………………… one of the men who killed him.

e Dian hates it when tourists come and …………………… the gorillas.

f The tourists are sometimes frightened that the gorillas will …………………… at them.

g Dian thinks that the tourists will give …………………… to the gorillas that will kill them.

h Ian is worried that Dian will make the Rwandan …………………… angry and that they will make things harder for her.

i Dian's friends at the US …………………… in Rwanda say that she should leave Karisoke for a while.

j Dian can't walk very well because her …………………… hurts a lot.

2 **What are the extra letters in the monkey? Write them in order, and find the name of Digit's daughter (born three months after he died).**

M _ _ _ _

GUESS WHAT

What do you think happens in the last chapter?
Tick three sentences.

a ☐ Dian and Alexie get married.

b ☐ Dian becomes a university professor.

c ☐ Dian finishes her book.

d ☐ Dian meets Bob Campbell again.

e ☐ Dian never goes back to Karisoke.

f ☐ Dian goes to study orang-utans in Borneo.

g ☐ Dian is killed in Africa.

h ☐ Dian dies in New York, a happy old woman.

·CHAPTER 10·
Gorillas in the mist

Dian and her dog Cindy moved into a small **apartment** in Ithaca, New York, near Cornell University. After a few weeks she went to a doctor who looked at her carefully.

Dian told him how difficult climbing was for her. 'Am I dying?'

'Well,' he said, 'your lungs are bad, but you're not dying. And there's a doctor in Canada who could help your back and hip.'

'I have to write my book. I don't want to go to Canada.'

'Well, that's for you to decide. Perhaps if you stop smoking, you'll feel better,' he said.

'I'll feel better when I don't have to worry about the most beautiful animals in the world,' she answered.

Dian never stopped worrying about the gorillas. As well as getting ready for her **lectures**, she was writing letters to get more money for *The Digit Fund*. But, at Cornell, she felt sure of herself. She was a professor, not a student. Her classes were full. Her students sat still as trees, as they listened to her. And she had time to write.

When the book was finished, she sent it to Anita, her **editor**. She knew Anita would like it; there was so much information in it. Everything was there, even what you can learn from gorilla dung. She named the book *Gorillas in the Mist*.

Dian was feeling better now. Because she wasn't up in the mountains, she could breathe easily. She had been to see the doctor in Canada, and he had helped a lot. She was smoking less and eating well. And now the book was finished.

Dian was in her apartment one evening when Anita called to say, 'I think we should meet soon.'

'Is this what you say to someone who just finished a book for you?' said Dian. 'What about "**Congratulations**!"?'

apartment a number of rooms in a larger building where someone lives

lecture a talk to a lot of students at a university

editor someone who changes a book to make it better

congratulations well done

'Well, congratulations on finishing the **first draft**.'

'First draft? You didn't like it?'

'Look, Dian. The book's great if I want to know everything about gorillas. But not everyone is interested in gorilla dung.'

'Well, they should be!' Dian almost hung up the telephone. This was her life's work. No editor was going to change it.

'There has to be more feeling in it, more of you.'

'There's too much of me already. This book is about them.'

'But how did you learn about them, Dian? How did you find out all of this? The mountain gorillas almost let you live with them. The first person to do that!'

'I didn't live with them. I watched them and listened to them. I was patient and they let me study them. Every night I wrote notes about what I saw and I used the notes in this book.'

In the end, Anita asked Dian to come with her to the offices of the National Geographic Society in Washington, DC. She told Dian she wanted her to choose photographs for the book. But really she was hoping the pictures would change Dian. So they found themselves in a room with hundreds of photographs on a table in front of them. 'What do you think? We can use maybe fifteen or twenty pictures,' said Anita.

For a minute, Dian couldn't talk. She hadn't looked at these photographs for some time. Now with the photographs in front of her, she told Anita what it was like to be accepted by the gorillas. She told her about Peanuts touching her and running away. She told her about Digit and how he liked to play with her camera. She talked about Nemeye and the other Africans who helped her. When she saw the pictures of her students, she told Anita how some could not live with the wet and the cold, while some stayed for years and helped her with the poachers.

'Please, Dian, write all of this in your book! If you want people to understand the gorillas, they have to understand what happened to the people who knew them.'

'I'll think about it,' was all Dian said.

first draft a book as a writer first writes it, without any of the editor's changes in it

In the end, Dian did write about Digit and Peanuts and the other gorillas, but she also wrote about people, those who were friends of the animals and those who weren't. On the first page, it said, 'To the memory of Digit, Uncle Bert, Macho and Kweli.' Anita was happy with the new draft.

Dian's time at Cornell was a success. Her students voted her 'Teacher of the Year'. She gave lectures with Jane Goodall and Birute Galdikas, Dr Leakey's two other 'ape women'.

But, during 1982, Dian continued to hear bad news from Karisoke. Another zoo wanted a baby gorilla and at least ten other gorillas were killed trying to capture it. Many tourists were paying to see the gorillas. Dian hated this although others thought it was necessary to bring money to Rwanda. Dian stayed up nights wondering where she could do the most good – staying in the United States, telling people about the gorillas and *The Digit Fund*, or going back to Karisoke to protect them?

When she heard about the capture of another young gorilla for a zoo she decided to return. Maybe with money from *The Digit Fund* she could stop the poachers and get rid of the tourists. In June 1983, she flew back to Africa, alone. Her dog Cindy had died the year before.

It didn't usually rain in June, but Dian arrived in the middle of a storm. 'Nothing has changed,' she thought as she climbed the steep trail up to Karisoke. Nemeye was the first to see her. He ran over to her, laughing and crying at the same time and put his arms around her. 'Now everything will be fine!' he said.

The others came out slowly. Dian had to laugh. She could tell they weren't sure it was her. 'It's OK,' she said. 'It's me – there's just more of me! I'm a little fatter!'

She spent the day talking to everyone. They all had stories to tell her. They told her about their families and their new babies. But not all the news was happy. Someone had broken into her cabin and stolen her cooking things and just about everything else. And the trackers still had to destroy hundreds of traps every year.

⚶ ⚶ ⚶

It took Dian a week to clean up her cabin. She missed her little monkey Kima who had died while she was gone, and she missed Cindy. But the Africans in the camp were happy to have her back.

Finally she was ready to go see the gorillas. How much could gorillas remember, she wondered. Would they know who she was? She had been away three years. It was too much to hope for.

The day was warm and sunny. A new tracker told her that Group 5 was nearby. They started out, but soon she was tired; climbing was still difficult. And then Dian realized this tracker did not know his way. She tried to help.

'Perhaps they're a little south of . . .' she stopped.

Just like the first time she was in the Virunga Mountains, she smelled that wonderful thick gorilla smell. Like Sanwekwe did so long ago, with her hands, she told the tracker to be quiet. She crawled through the bushes toward the smell. Some gorillas were in their day nests on the side of the mountain. Some were eating. She saw one, then another. She counted them – sixteen in all, no males, just females and their babies.

With her head down, making the *naroom* sounds, that she learned so long ago, she knuckle-walked until she was about six metres away from them. One of the babies came over to look at her camera. Dian was angry. Look, she thought. This baby doesn't know me but because she has seen lots of tourists, she feels safe. What will the mothers do?

Then Effie, the baby's mother, saw her. Dian had known Effie almost fifteen years. Would she **attack**? Dian wondered. Then Tuck, another gorilla that Dian had known since she was a baby, saw her. Both came running over. Dian was a bit frightened.

Tuck walked right up to Dian and looked in her face. Dian waited. Tuck stared at her. Ten seconds, twenty seconds, thirty seconds. Dian lay down, showing her stomach. 'Please, don't

attack to start fighting

growl. Please don't be afraid of me,' she thought.

Tuck bent down and smelled Dian. First her hair, then her neck. And then she lay down next to Dian, put her arms around her and stayed there. By this time Effie was on Dian's other side. Soon all sixteen of the group were around her. Dian was home.

That night, with tears in her eyes, she wrote in her diary,

I could have died right then and there and wished for nothing more in this world because they remembered.

Dian Fossey lived at Karisoke for two more years. During that time her students and staff cut down hundreds of traps. Her book *Gorillas in the Mist* was published in the summer of 1983.

Dian with her book

On December 27, 1985 Dian Fossey was killed as she slept in her cabin. No one knows who did it; even today it is still a mystery. She had made many enemies as she tried to protect the only mountain gorillas left in the world.

Dian was buried in a grave next to Digit and the other gorillas. On her grave, it says;

Nyiramachabelli
Dian Fossey
1932–1985
No one loved gorillas more

Through her work, and the work of her students, much is known about the mountain gorillas. Because Dian started her war against the poachers, there are more gorillas today than when she first arrived, and students still go to Karisoke to study. There is less poaching in the Virunga Mountains, but sadly it still happens.

The Digit Fund now has a new name – *The Dian Fossey Gorilla Fund* – in **memory** of the woman who did so much to help the mountain gorillas. If you are interested in learning more about it, you can find it on the Internet at www.gorillas.org.

To help the Rwandan people, tourists are allowed to visit the gorillas. The park officials make sure people who are sick cannot visit them.

A film, *Gorillas in the Mist*, was made about Dian's life in 1988. Sigourney Weaver, an American actress, played the part of Dian.

memory what you remember

READING CHECK

Are these sentences true or false? Tick the boxes.

		True	False
a	Dian and her monkey go to live in New York.	☐	☑
b	Dian goes to see a doctor about her back and her hip.	☐	☐
c	She becomes a student at Cornell University.	☐	☐
d	She has lots of time to write her book.	☐	☐
e	Once Dian finishes her book Anita wants to make changes in it.	☐	☐
f	When Dian goes to choose photos for the book she talks about her life with the gorillas.	☐	☐
g	Anita asks Dian not to put stories about the people who helped her in her book.	☐	☐
h	Dian goes back to Africa with her dog Cindy to help the gorillas.	☐	☐
i	The people at Karisoke are happy to have Dian back with them.	☐	☐
j	Dian is angry when the gorillas from Group 5 come very near to her.	☐	☐
k	Dian Fossey was killed one day when she was looking for poachers in the mountains.	☐	☐

WORD WORK

Use the definitions to complete the crossword on page 71 with new words from Chapter 10.

a a person whose job is to help write a book

b what you say when someone does something good

c to begin fighting

d something that you remember

e a number of rooms together in a larger building

f a talk at a university that lots of students listen to

g a book the way that a writer first writes it

WHAT NEXT?

1 What do you think will happen in the future? Tick the boxes.

In 2050 . . .

a ☐ there will be no gorillas alive.

b ☐ there will be some gorillas alive, but only in zoos.

c ☐ there will still be a few gorillas living in Rwanda.

d ☐ there will be a lot of gorillas living in national parks in Africa.

e ☐ lots of people will be 'gorilla tourists'.

f ☐ there will be no 'gorilla tourists'.

2 Talk about your ideas with a partner.

PROJECT A *Two-sided diaries*

1 Read a page that could be from Dian's diary. Which page in the story is it from?

Earlier this evening I was writing my notes in my tent when I heard a friendly voice behind me. 'Who's this?' it asked. I knew it was Alexie's voice and I turned round, but I couldn't speak for a while. I got up and said 'What are you doing here?' I hadn't heard him come into the tent, and he hadn't written me to say he was coming to see me. 'That's a nice way to say hello!' he laughed. Oh, dear! I can understand gorillas so well, but it's when I have to talk to people that I have problems. Alexie looked at the photo of Digit. Is he jealous of my feelings for the gorillas? Of the time that I spend here in Africa with them? 'That's one of my gorillas. I call him Digit.' I explained But we couldn't talk longer because at that moment there was a lot of noise outside the tent.

2 Use these notes to write a diary page by Alexie about the same moment in the story.

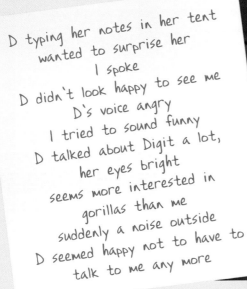

D typing her notes in her tent
wanted to surprise her
I spoke
D didn't look happy to see me
D's voice angry
I tried to sound funny
D talked about Digit a lot,
her eyes bright
seems more interested in
gorillas than me
suddenly a noise outside
D seemed happy not to have to
talk to me any more

3 Now write another two diary pages – one by Dian and one by someone she meets in another part of the story. Choose from these people.

Dr Leakey

Sanwekwe
. . .

ALAN & JOAN ROOT

Bob Campbell

Alyette de Munck

Michael (the student from California)

PROJECT B   *An African country*

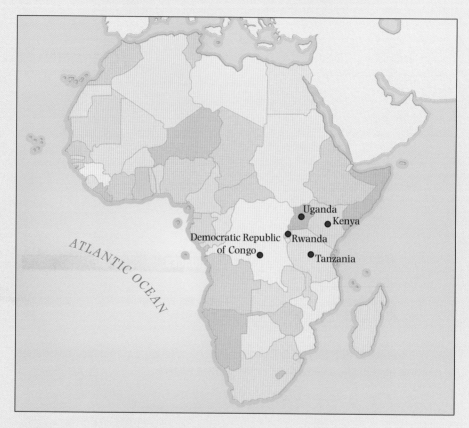

1 **Look at the map of the African countries in this book. Complete the sentences with the country names.**

   a The Leakeys were looking for giraffe bones in ....

   b Dian first met mountain gorillas in ....

   c When Dian went to live in Africa, Dr Leakey met her at the airport in the capital of
   ....

   d When there was fighting in the Congo, Dian escaped first to .... and then
   went to see Dr Leakey in Nairobi.

   e Dian started her second gorilla research camp in ....

2 Read the text and complete the information table.

★ The Democratic Republic of Congo is in Central Africa. The capital is Kinshasa. It is a very big country — 2,345,410 square kilometres in size. It used to be a Belgian colony, but it became an independent country in 1960. French is the official language but people there speak African languages like Lingala and Swahili, too. There are a number of National Parks in the country — including Garamba, Kahuzi-Biega, Virunga and Salouge — where you can see rhinoceros, elephants, giraffes, gorillas, lions, chimpanzees, duikers, monkeys and other animals. The Democratic Republic of Congo exports copper, diamonds and oil to other countries. The Polish-born writer, Joseph Conrad, wrote about the Congo in his story *Heart of Darkness*.

NAME:		LANGUAGES:
LOCATION:		**NATIONAL PARKS:**
CAPITAL:		**ANIMALS:**
AREA:	sq km	
COLONIZED BY:		**EXPORTS:**
INDEPENDENCE:		**WRITER:**

3 Look at the tables on page 76 and write about another African country. Use the text above about the Democratic Republic of Congo to help you.

NAME:

Republic of Kenya

LOCATION:

East Africa

CAPITAL:

Nairobi

AREA:

582,645 sq km

COLONIZED BY:

Britain

INDEPENDENCE:

12 December 1963

LANGUAGES:

English, Gikuyu, Swahili

NATIONAL PARKS:

Aberdares, Amboseli, Lake Nakuru

ANIMALS:

elephants, leopards, black rhinos, ostriches, flamingos, white rhinos

EXPORTS:

tea, coffee

WRITER:

Karen Blixen, Danish-born — book *Out of Africa*

NAME:

Republic of Uganda

LOCATION:

East Africa

CAPITAL:

Kampala

AREA:

286,040 sq km

COLONIZED BY:

Britain

INDEPENDENCE:

9 October 1963

LANGUAGES:

English, Swahili

NATIONAL PARKS:

Bwindi, Kibele Forest, Kidepo, Murchison

ANIMALS:

mountain gorillas, chimpanzees, monkeys, lions, ostriches, crocodiles

EXPORTS:

coffee, cotton, tea

WRITER:

Peter Nazareth, Ugandan-born — novel *The General is Up*

NAME:

United Republic of Tanzania

LOCATION:

East Africa

CAPITAL:

Dodoma

AREA:

945,090 sq km

COLONIZED BY:

Britain

INDEPENDENCE:

9 December 1961

LANGUAGES:

Swahili, English

NATIONAL PARKS:

Arusha, Katavi, Lake Manyara, Mahale Mountains

ANIMALS:

elephants, monkeys, zebras, lions, hippos, chimpanzees

EXPORTS:

coffee, cotton

WRITER:

Moyez G Vassanji, Kenyan-born — novel *The Book of Secrets*

GRAMMAR CHECK

Infinitive of purpose

We can use the infinitive with *to* to talk about why we do something.

Dian learned Swahili to help her work in the Congo.

One of the students stayed at Karisoke to take care of the camp.

1 Match the sentence halves.

a Alyette argued with Dian   1 to get money for the park.

b Alexie went to Africa   2 to marry Dian and take her away.

c The Park Director sold Coco to a zoo   3 to offer her a job.

d Dian kidnapped Munyarukiko's son   4 to scare the poachers.

e Dr Leakey wrote to Diane   5 to stop her destroying the traps.

2 Complete the sentences. Use *to* and the verbs in the box.

teach	make	take	~~save~~	study	discuss	take

a Ian thought of a fund to get money .....to save.... the gorillas.

b The Chief of Police came to Karisoke .... Digit's killer away.

c Anita met Dian .... her book with her.

d Bob Campbell went to Karisoke ....
photos of gorillas.

e People cut off the hands and heads of gorillas
.... things to show to their friends.

f Dian went to Cambridge .... for a
doctorate.

g Later, she went to Cornell University in New York
....

77

GRAMMAR CHECK

Past Perfect: affirmative and negative

We use the Past Perfect when we are already talking about the past (using the Past Simple) and we want to talk about an action that happened earlier in the past, before the Past Simple action. To make the Past Perfect, we use had/hadn't + past participle.

Dian hadn't met wild gorillas before she visited the Virunga mountains.

Dian found some cows eating where Group 5 had been the day before.

We can use never with the Past Perfect to give extra emphasis to a statement.

Dian had never been this happy in all her life.

3 **Complete Dian's diary. Use the Past Simple or Past Perfect form of the verbs in brackets.**

I a) ...woke... (wake) up early this morning. I b) .... (not sleep) very well during the night, and I c) .... (feel) tired. I d) .... (decide) to go to look for Group 5 near the river. I e) .... (know) that they f) .... (be) there two days earlier.
When I g) .... (get) there, the gorillas h) .... (not be) there. But someone from the village i) .... (make) a trap there, and a duiker j) .... (fall) into it. It k) .... (break) its leg. I l) .... (feel) very angry, because the little animal m) .... (be) in pain.
When I n) .... (get) back to the camp, a packet was waiting for me. It o) .... (arrive) from Bob. He p) .... (send) me some copies of the latest National Geographic magazine, with lots of the photos he q) .... (take) of Coco and Pucker in it. I r) .... (never see) such wonderful photos before. I s) .... (show) them to two of the students. They t) .... (never know) Coco, but they u) .... (like) the photos.
That night I v) .... (go) to bed happy. I w) .... (have) a difficult morning, but Bob's photos x) .... (make) me feel better.

GRAMMAR CHECK

Time clauses with until, since, and as

We can use the conjunctions until, since and as with time clauses that refer to the past. We use until + Past Simple to talk about something that happened in the past to end an earlier situation.

Dian worked at the hospital until Dr Leakey offered her a job.

We use Present Perfect + since + Past Simple to talk about the starting point of a past situation that continues to the present.

The Digit Fund has collected money for gorillas since Digit died.

We can use as + Past Simple to talk about something that happened in the middle of another past action.

As Dian showed the mask to the porter, he ran screaming from the tent.

4 Complete Dian's letter with *until*, *since,* or *as*.

> Dear Mom and Dad,
>
> a) ..Since.. I last wrote to you things have changed. I wanted to stay in Kabara Meadow, but it was not possible. The Director told me that I had to go. I cried b) .... I came down the mountain.
>
> I could not go to Uganda c) .... the fighting stopped. When I met Dr Leakey there, he had a new plan for me – studying orang-utans! d) .... he told me about his plans, I told him about my plans – to go to Volcanoes National Park in Rwanda. And now I am here, at a place called Karisoke. I searched e) .... I found some new gorilla dung, and then I knew I was in the right place. I've been at Karisoke f) .... the porters brought my tents up, and I'm going to make a camp here. g) .... I arrived I have followed a new group of gorillas. There is a young male in the group who is very playful. h) .... I watched him one day I saw that he had a damaged finger, so I have named him Digit. An older gorilla called Uncle Bert looks after the group. Yesterday Uncle Bert tickled Digit i) .... Digit ran away.
> Love,
> *Dian*

GRAMMAR CHECK

So and neither

We can use so or neither in conversations to agree with something that someone has just said. We use so to agree with an affirmative sentence.

Louis Leakey is an anthropologist. So is Mary. (= Mary is, too.)

We use neither to agree with a negative sentence.

Coco didn't have a mother. Neither did Pucker. (= Pucker didn't, either.)

We use so/neither + auxiliary verb/main verb *be* + subject.

The gorillas live in the forest. So do the duikers.

Dian was a teacher. So was Alan.

5 Write sentences. Use *so* or *neither* and the words in brackets.

a Digit was killed by the poachers. (Uncle Bert, too.)

.................................So was Uncle Bert.............................

b Coco went to live in a zoo. (Pucker, too.)

....

c In the end, Alexie did not stay with Dian. (Not Bob, either.)

....

d Dian could not sleep after Digit died. (Not Ian, either.)

....

e Karisoke is rainy, cold and beautiful. (Kabara Meadow, too.)

....

f The Park Director was not afraid of Dian. (Not the poachers, either.)

....

g Dian scratched her head and neck. (Peanuts, too.)

....

h Students wanted to come to Karisoke. (Tourists, too.)

....

i Digit's grave is in Karisoke. (Dian's grave, too.)

....

GRAMMAR CHECK

Linkers: but and although

We use but and although to show that one idea in a sentence is in contrast with another. But usually goes between two clauses.

Dian liked the fruit and vegetables in England, but she hated being a student again.

Although can go at the beginning of the first clause or the second clause in a sentence.

Although Dian liked the fruit and vegetables in England, she hated being a student again.

Dian hated being a student again, although she liked the fruit and vegetables in England.

6   Match the sentence halves.

a The Roots took photographs,

b Dian had travelled many miles in Africa,

c Although Dian didn't tell anyone,

d Although it was hard to climb with a heavy bag,

e Dian had not seen Alexie in over a year,

f Although Coco and Pucker were feeling better,

g Bob loved making the film about the gorillas,

h Bob was waiting for Digit to run away,

i Ian felt the same as Dian,

1 Dian was tired after taking care of them for a month.

2 she was always afraid of being high up.

3 but the young gorilla lay down next to Dian.

4 but Dian just stared at the gorillas.

5 but his life was not in Karisoke.

6 Dian carried everything she needed with her.

7 although he didn't like everything she did in Karisoke.

8 but she was not ready to go home yet.

9 although they had written to each other.

GRAMMAR CHECK

Gerund and infinitive

After some verbs – such as enjoy, finish, and love – we use the gerund (–ing form).

Dian enjoyed speaking to people in Los Angeles about the gorillas.

We also use the gerund after some adjectives, such as worth.

It's not worth trying to stop the poachers.

After some verbs – such as decide, hope, need, and promise – we use the infinitive + to.

Bob decided to leave Karisoke when the film was finished.

We also use (not) + to + infinitive after tell + noun/pronoun.

Ian told Dian not to kidnap the boy.

We can miss out the second *to* when two infinitives follow the same verb.

We need to stop the poachers and (to) find more money to help the gorillas.

After some verbs – such as begin, continue, and start – we can use either the gerund or the infinitive + *to*, without changing the meaning.

7 A tourist has written a report about a journey to see gorillas. Complete the text with the correct form of the verbs in brackets.

We arrived at the village late in the afternoon. We talked to the park ranger, and he promised a) ..to take.. us to see the gorillas. We all hoped b) ....
(see) these extraordinary animals and c) .... (take) photos of them. Next morning we got up early and started d) .... (walk) while it was cool. I love e) .... (walk), but it was very tiring. We continued f) .... (climb) for hours into the forests where the gorillas live.

At 11 o'clock we all needed g) .... (rest), because it was hot and we were exhausted. We enjoyed h) .... (sit) under the trees and i) ....
(have) a cold drink. Then we set off again. Suddenly the ranger told us j) .... (be) quiet. There were six gorillas! When we finished k) .... (take) photos, we walked back down to the village again. Was it worth l) .... (climb) up the mountain for four hours to see them? Yes, it certainly was!

GRAMMAR CHECK

Relative clauses with who, which, that, where, and when

We use who or that to introduce relative clauses about people.

Michael was the first student who/that came to Karisoke.

We use which or that to introduce relative clauses about things.

Digit was the first Group 4 gorilla which/that Dian named.

We use where to introduce relative clauses about places.

Kabara Meadow was the place where Dian saw her first wild gorillas.

We use when to introduce relative clauses about times.

Dr Leakey remembered the morning when he first met Dian.

We do not use commas with this kind of relative clause because the sentence is not complete without it.

8 **Complete these sentences with *who, which, that, where* or *when*.**

a They went to the group of trees ...*where*... Peanuts first showed his trust in Dian.

b Tourists can bring in diseases .... will kill the gorillas.

c *Gorillas in the Mist* was the name of the book .... Dian wrote.

d Alan was the schoolteacher .... had sat next to Dian in Cambridge.

e Bob's photo showed the moment .... Peanuts put his hand in Dian's hand.

f Dian used the masks .... Alexie sent her to scare the poachers.

g Munyarukiko was the poacher .... tried to kill the Group 5 gorillas.

h Los Angeles was the place .... Dian gave her first talk about the gorillas.

i Bob remembered the sad day .... Coco and Pucker had to leave Karisoke.

j Sanwekwe showed Dian the fresh dung .... the gorillas had left.

k The poachers made pits .... they covered with leaves.

l Alyette was the woman .... helped Dian in Rwanda.

m Cornell was the university .... Dian was voted 'Teacher of the Year'.

n June 1983 was the month .... Dian flew back to Africa to stop the poachers and get rid of the tourists.

Dominoes is an enjoyable series of illustrated classic and modern stories in four carefully graded language stages – from Starter to Three – which take learners from beginner to intermediate level.

Each *Domino* reader includes:

- **a good story** to read and enjoy
- **integrated activities** to develop reading skills and increase active vocabulary
- **personalized projects** to make the language and story themes more meaningful
- **seven pages of grammar activities** for consolidation.

Each *Domino* pack contains a reader, plus a MultiROM with:

- **a complete audio recording of the story**, fully dramatized to bring it to life
- **interactive activities** to offer further practice in reading and language skills and to consolidate learning.

If you liked this Level Three *Domino*, why not read these?

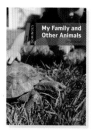

My Family and Other Animals
Gerald Durrell

The weather in England that summer had been so awful that Gerald's mother sold the family house and took her children to live on the Mediterranean island of Corfu. Between lessons, the ten-year-old Gerald was free to walk round the sunny island and discover the wonderful people and animals living there.

This is the story of Gerald's adventures with the fascinating animals of Corfu, and, of course, with his surprising family and their friends.

Book ISBN: 978 0 19 424824 2
MultiROM Pack ISBN: 978 0 19 424782 5

The Moonstone
Wilkie Collins

The Moonstone is a beautiful yellow diamond that was stolen from the statue of a Moon god in India. When Franklin Blake brings it to Rachel Verinder's house in Yorkshire for her birthday, it brings bad luck with it.

How many people will the Moonstone hurt? How many must die before the diamond's revenge is complete

Book ISBN: 978 0 19 424821 1
MultiROM Pack ISBN: 978 0 19 424779 5

You can find details and a full list of books in the *Dominoes* catalogue and Oxford English Language Teaching Catalogue, and on the website: www.oup.com/elt

Teachers: see www.oup.com/elt for a full range of online support, or consult your local office.

	CEF	Cambridge Exams	IELTS	TOEFL iBT	TOEIC
Starter	A1	YLE Movers	–	–	–
Level 1	A1–A2	YLE Flyers/KET	3.0	–	–
Level 2	A2–B1	KET-PET	3.0-4.0	–	–
Level 3	B1	PET	4.0	57-86	550